CONTEMPORARY BRITAIN

Ruth Blakey M.A.

formerly Principal Teacher of Modern Studies,
Craigbank Secondary School, Glasgow

Wilson Blakey M.A.(Hons) Dip. Ed.

Principal Teacher of Modern Studies,
Waverley Secondary School, Glasgow

Bob McKay B.A.(Hons)

formerly Principal Teacher of Modern Studies,
now Assistant Head Teacher
St Augustine's Secondary School, Glasgow

Oliver & Boyd

Contents

Introduction

The study of contemporary Britain – our country in the present day – is complicated. A glance at the contents page will show the wide variety of topics to be covered.

The authors have arranged material in three parts and in each part they try to show how the individual is involved in the working of contemporary Britain.

Part 1 Politics

Politics is the study of why and how societies reach decisions. Societies can be small groups of people, members of a club, a gang, neighbours or large groups such as a local community or a whole nation. Nearly everyone in Britain over the age of eighteen is entitled to vote and if they do not choose to vote or do so without careful thought, then they can hardly criticise those who have been chosen by those who did vote.

Part 2 Economics

Economics is the study of how and why societies make use of things they make or acquire. Britain is a major trading and manufacturing nation and it is important to know how goods are made and used because we are all producers and consumers in some way.

Part 3 Society

Society is made up of different individuals and groups. We are all members of different groups – family, school, factory workforce, village, town, city, region, nation. Wherever people are gathered together there may be disagreements, arguments, and disputes. A way has to be found to settle these conflicts and to reach agreement on some form of co-operation. It is hard to escape being involved in society.

In this way the authors illustrate the fact that people do not live in isolation from each other and the rest of the world. Our actions and decisions affect other people, who in turn want to help us to be healthy, teach us things, make things for us, sell us things, stop us hurting ourselves or others, and give advice or assistance when it is needed.

No book is large enough to include a complete picture of life in Britain today. However, the authors have collected a wide variety of material for the reader to study: straight text giving information and explanation; photographs; diagrams to help with the understanding of ideas and relationships; graphs and tables giving facts and statistics; and simulation case studies (short stories or descriptions of imaginary people in real situations).

To this information the reader and/or teacher should add other resources which are similar or different to those in the book. Finally the whole mass of information should be compared with and added to the reader's own experience. This is a source book. Choose the bits you find valuable and use the questions included as a check on whether you do have an understanding of contemporary Britain.

PART 1

Politics

British Government

Introduction

Britain is widely regarded as having a democratic system of government. That is to say, the British people have a say in how the country should be run. The reader will be able to decide in the next few pages to what extent this statement is true. No country allows its people to take all the decisions all the time, sometimes because it is not physically possible to ask their opinion, and sometimes because the country is run by a dictator or by an elite group who are not interested in the opinions of the people. The British system falls somewhere between.

A system of governing a country which does claim to be democratic allows for disagreements and argument, usually on the understanding that once a decision has been taken, the minority will allow the majority to rule in return for some concessions. Thus there is frequent conflict as to how to choose a government and what the government should be allowed to do once chosen. The study of British government can be difficult, partly because many of its rules are unwritten **conventions** and partly because it is complicated. By following the fortunes of two imaginary politicians, its study can be made less difficult.

General Election Special

Today, Thursday, 29th October, is **election** day throughout the United Kingdom. The **polls** closed just a short time ago at 10 p.m. This marks the climax of a three-week campaign. We are now going over to our political reporter, James Neil, to see how the campaign and results have gone in Newtown, Scotland.

'Good evening, and welcome to the packed Newtown Town Hall where the count is taking place. While we are waiting for the result let me explain what the election has meant to the people of Newtown. There are two constituencies, one a safe Labour seat, and the other a marginal held narrowly by the Conservatives at the last election. Since 7 a.m. this morning, workers of all parties have been making sure their promised voters have gone to the poll. It looks as if it will be a very close contest in Newtown South constituency. No party

Voting

POLLING STATION

PRESIDING OFFICER

ELECTORAL REGISTER

VOTING BOOTH

ANDERSON, PETER Conservative Party
JONES, ANDREW Labour Party
MORRISON, MARY Liberal Party
YOUNG, HUGH Scottish National Party

BALLOT BOX

PARTY SUPPORTERS

BALLOT PAPER

is sure of victory. In the last five elections the majority has never been greater than 2000. The Conservative candidate, James Falconer, is a young local estate agent who has campaigned mainly on price rises and local issues. Hugh Daly is a trade union official sponsored by that union as Labour **candidate**. The other two candidates are James Rodgers, Liberal, and Mary Thomson, Scottish National Party. There are suggestions that the vote will be so close that a recount may be required.

In Newtown North the sitting MP, Peter Brown, is again contesting the seat for Labour. He has been the Member of Parliament here since his win in a by-election sixteen years ago. He is also a member of the Cabinet. His main opponent, Mr Wharton, Conservative, has led a vigorous campaign, but it would require a massive swing to unseat Mr Brown from this very safe Labour constituency. Of the other three opponents, Stuart Armstrong, SNP, Harold Dawson, Liberal and Peter Webster, Independent, the predictions are that only the SNP candidate has a chance of saving his **deposit**.

Both constituencies have had a very heavy poll — nearly eighty per cent.

It will be some time before the results are announced. And so I have this opportunity to talk to

Campaigning

 Members of the Royal Family

 Members of the House of Lords

 Convicted criminals and inmates of mental institutions

 British citizens on holiday abroad

two of the main contestants in Newtown, Mr Brown and Mr Falconer.'

Neil Mr Brown, the national opinion polls suggest that you may well be returning with your party to government. Are you hoping to be back in the Cabinet?

Brown Well, Mr Neil, the Prime Minister decides on his Cabinet, but I would agree that the Labour Party will have an overall majority in the House of Commons.

Falconer I would not accept that. My own canvas returns in South constituency clearly point to a Conservative victory and I believe that the Conservative Party nationally will not only hold safe seats but will win marginals such as my own.

Neil As a first time candidate, Mr Falconer, might I ask you how you see your role as an MP?

Falconer If elected, I would look forward to representing all the people of Newtown South constituency and participating as a backbench MP in a Conservative government.

Neil Mr Brown, as a man who has successfully fought many campaigns what changes have you noticed in campaigns over the years?

Brown Some things like canvassing, leafleting, public meetings and hard work never change, but in recent years television, radio and public opinion polls have played an increasing part.

Neil Thank you very much, gentlemen, I believe you now have to return to the Town Hall as the Returning Officer is about to announce the results in both constituencies.

'I, James Morris, being the Returning Officer for the constituencies of Newtown North and South, declare that the total number of votes cast for each candidate in Newtown North was as follows:

Armstrong, Stuart	11 923
Brown, Peter	23 506
Dawson, Harold	3 704
Webster, Peter	208
Wharton, Nigel	12 047

I therefore declare that the said Peter Brown has been elected to serve as Member of Parliament for the Newtown North constituency.

The returning officer, the Mayor, reads the results of the 1974 election, when Mr Edward Heath held his Sidcup seat.

. . . in the Newtown South constituency was as follows:

Daly, Hugh	15 417
Falconer, James	15 742
Rodgers, James	4 029
Thomson, Mary	9 418
Spoiled papers	27

and I declare that . . .'

'Before returning you to the studio let me sum up. Labour have held their safe seat. The Conservatives have held their marginal with a reduced majority. The SNP on their first attempt have come third in both constituencies. Both the Liberal candidates and the Independent have lost their £150 deposit since none received an eighth of the total vote in their constituency. And now back to the studio for the national results.'

Election Results

Reporter With only a few results to come, none of which are likely to change hands, we can predict with some certainty that the final result will be:

Labour	320 MPs
Conservative	286 MPs
Others	29 MPs

A very small swing to the Labour party means that the Queen will be inviting the leader of the Labour party to form a government. The overall majority is five.

We have in the studio representatives of the Labour, Conservative, Liberal and SNP parties.

Ladies and gentlemen, can I ask you for your first reactions?

Labour spokesman Well, we are delighted to have won and although the overall majority is only five the opposition is not united and we do have a majority of thirty-four over our nearest rivals.

Conservative spokesman I think another election within eighteen months is very likely since the new government's majority is so small.

Liberal spokesman This election again demonstrates the basic unfairness of the British electoral system. The Labour and Conservative Parties each have thirty-nine per cent of the total **vote** cast, yet Labour have more than fifty per cent of the seats, and Conservatives have well over forty per cent of the seats. The Liberals and other smaller parties have fewer seats than the national vote entitles them to.

SNP spokesman I must agree with the last speaker. The two major parties support the present voting system only because they benefit from its unfairness.

Labour spokesman That is hardly true. We support the present system because it is easy to operate, understood by the **electorate** and it is democratic. Furthermore, it provides for stability and continuity of government and avoids the type of coalitions to be found in other Western European states.

Reporter Perhaps we can look at alternative voting systems and examine the possible effects on parties and government in the UK.

Table 1 Election Results since 1966

Year	Labour		Conservative		Liberal		Others	
	Seats	% votes	Seats	% votes	Seats	% votes	Seats	% votes
1966	363	48	253	42	12	9	2	1
1970	287	43	330	46	6	7	7 (SNP 3)	3
Feb '74	301	38	296	39	14	19	24 (SNP 7)	4
Oct '74	319	39	276	36	13	18	27 (SNP 11)	7
1979	268	37	339	44	11	14	17 (SNP 2)	4

Voting Systems

The present system is the 'simple majority' or 'first past the post' system. The voter puts a cross on the ballot paper beside the name of the candidate of his/her choice and the candidate receiving more votes than any other single candidate in each constituency wins. If you look at the two results in Newtown, you will note that neither winner received fifty per cent or more of the total vote cast. This system tends to favour the two major parties.

The supporters of a change in the voting system, e.g. the Liberal Party, point to statistics such as those of the 1974 (February) election:
a) the Labour Party won five more seats (and formed a government) with one per cent fewer votes than the Conservatives.
b) the total votes cast for each party divided by the number of seats gained, show that the Liberals had approximately one seat per 400 000 voters, whereas Labour and Conservative had one seat per 40–60 000 voters.

PROPORTIONAL REPRESENTATION

Proportional representation is any electoral system which would try to distribute the seats in the House of Commons between the parties in a way which ensured that the percentage of seats for each party more closely reflected the percentage of votes cast for each party. The following table demonstrates the change in seat distribution which would have taken place in February 1974 under one of the systems of proportional representation.

Table 2 February, 1974

	Labour	Conservative	Liberal	Others
Actual seats	301	296	14	24
Prop. rep. seats	236	241	123	35

The following are two methods of proportional representation.

Alternative Vote

In this system, if there are more than two candidates, the voter numbers them in his/her order of preference (1 for first choice, 2 for second choice). The first choices are then counted. If one candidate is the first choice of fifty per cent plus one of all voters, he/she is declared the winner. If no one has achieved this, the candidate coming last is eliminated and the second choices of the voters who supported him/her, are distributed among the other candidates. This process continues until one candidate has fifty per cent plus one of the votes.

The National List System

This requires each political party to provide a list of up to 635 candidates in order of preference. The electorate vote for the party of their choice rather than an individual candidate. On the basis of the total number of votes cast for each party nationally, the same percentage of seats in the House of Commons would be given to each party. For example, if the Liberal Party received twenty per cent of the national vote they would be given twenty per cent of the seats in the House of Commons. This would be about 120 seats and therefore the first 120 candidates on the Liberal list would become Members of Parliament.

Questions

1. Describe how you would go about voting, from walking in the polling station door, to walking out. 5
2. If you were a candidate, what would you do to try to win an election? 5
3. Why are some people not allowed to vote? 2
4. Describe, with as much detail as you can, the winning candidates in the two constituencies. 6
5. What are the advantages of the first past the post voting system? 3

The Parties

In the General Election several political parties were mentioned. We should therefore examine the parties, their principles and beliefs. The two major parties are the Conservative and Labour Parties, although in recent years they have lost some of their support to the minor parties: the Liberals, the Scottish and Welsh Nationalists and several other parties in Northern Ireland. Each party offers alternative proposals for Britain's **economic, political, social** and international development. The parties do not disagree on every issue, e.g. in foreign affairs the Labour and Conservative Parties are often in agreement. The major areas of disagreement are in social and economic matters. It should also be noted that each party is not itself totally united on every issue, and is made up of people with quite a wide range of ideas and beliefs.

THE LABOUR PARTY

The Labour Party has its origins in various working-class and intellectual movements of the late 19th and early 20th centuries. The different groups within the Party share the common goal of the redistribution of wealth by the taxation of the well-off, by government action. They do not always agree on the extent or type of action, however. The left wing of the party (e.g. the Tribune Group) are in favour of the public ownership of wealth on behalf of the working classes. The centre and right of the party (e.g. the Manifesto Group) prefer to pursue the redistribution of wealth by the taxation of private wealth.

The Labour Party in the 1920s became the alternative to the Conservatives and, in 1923 and 1929, formed short-lived minority governments. In 1945 they formed their first majority government and also won the 1950 election by a narrow majority. During this period they introduced considerable **nationalisation** and established the National Health Service. They were also in power between 1964 and 1970 and from 1974 to 1979.

Labour believe that government must play a major role in the economy, not only by public ownership, but also by control and regulation. They are more concerned with the ideas of the **community**, its needs and demands than with individual enterprise. Their ideal is a redistribution of wealth either by taxation or increased public ownership.

Some examples of the ideals of the Labour Party are:

Education A belief in **comprehensive** education for all and an abandonment of selective schools (Junior and Senior Secondaries) together with an unwillingness to support private schools.

Housing A tendency to support an expansion of the public sector, i.e. the building of local **authority** housing for rent. They have also been responsible for legislation to control private landlords.

Nationalisation In 1977 the Labour Government nationalised the British shipbuilding and ship repair industries. This was bitterly opposed by the Conservative Opposition.

THE CONSERVATIVE PARTY

The Conservative Party is the oldest major British political party. Today, like the Labour Party, it reflects a mixture of different philosophies with a common goal. It includes those who support completely free enterprise (business with little or no government interference) and others who accept some government responsibility but would not support the 'socialism' of the Labour Party.

Before 1945, the Conservative Party held power more often than any other party. Since 1945, their periods in power have been 1951 to 1964 and 1970 to 1974 and from 1979. The Conservative philosophy hinges on the support of the individual, free and private enterprise and a limited government role in the economy. In recent years this has expressed itself in their idea of 'choice'.

Education Although giving some support to comprehensive education, they have fought to retain selective schools and have argued for 'choice' within the comprehensive system.

Housing They are less inclined to support local authority housing and **subsidised** rents and favour large-scale council house sales and private house building.

Nationalisation Although they did not fully de-nationalise after 1951, they oppose the idea in principle.

THE LIBERAL PARTY

The parliamentary power of the Liberal Party has declined throughout this century. When the Labour Party became the accepted alternative party to the Conservatives, the Liberals began to lose ground and, since 1945, they have always had fewer than twenty MPs. The Liberal Party see themselves as a radical alternative to the two main parties. They oppose the ideas of public ownership but prefer profit-sharing schemes to complete private enterprise. They are strong supporters of individual and human rights, social reform, federalism and a complete reform of the tax system. Internationally, they were strongly in favour of UK membership of the EEC and they support NATO.

NATIONALIST PARTIES

Scottish and Welsh **Nationalists** are in favour of Scotland and Wales being separate states. They believe that Scotland and Wales are separate nations historically, economically and culturally, and that their interests are not best advanced by a UK parliament.

On the major social and economic issues they tend to be internally divided since they have within their membership people of socialist, conservative and liberal views.

From the late 1960s until the General Election of 1979 the Nationalists enjoyed a considerable electoral revival (see Table 1).

OTHER PARTIES

In addition to the parties described above, the voter may also choose to vote for one of the fringe parties (if they put up a candidate), such as the Communist Party, the Socialist Workers Party or the National Front.

The tradition of 'Independent' candidates has largely disappeared except at by-elections. One other choice for the elector, and one exercised by more than twenty per cent of the electorate at most general elections is to abstain, i.e. not to vote at all.

There are many areas in which most, if not all, major parties agree. Among the issues which the Conservative and Labour parties agree are 'bad things' are unemployment, inflation, terrorism, crime, discrimination and corruption.

Among the 'good things' on which they agree are fairness, a rising **standard of living**, Britain's membership of the EEC and NATO.

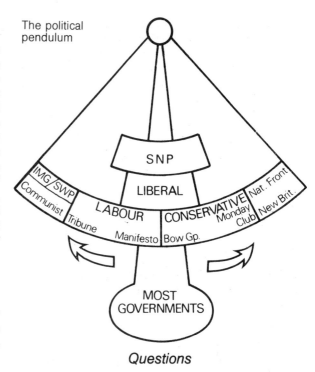

The political pendulum

Questions

1 What are the main aims of each of the four biggest parties?   8
2 What would the policies of the major parties be on a) unemployment b) housing c) defence d) capital punishment?   8
3 Using the pendulum, which parties would be described as extremists, and which as moderates?   3
4 What are the views of the Liberal Party and the SNP on major issues?   4

The House of Commons

Peter Brown and James Falconer have been elected to serve as members of the House of Commons. This is the elected House of **Parliament** with 635 members (until 1979).

Peter Brown, being a member of the party having a majority in the House of Commons, will sit on the benches to the right of the Speaker. (The Speaker is the MP who is Chairman of the House of Commons, elected by his fellow members and responsible for the conduct of business and **debate**. It is the Speaker who applies the rules, procedures and traditions of the House. He only votes when the 'ayes' and 'noes' tie.) Since Mr Brown has been selected by the Prime Minister to be Secretary of State for Scotland, he will occupy a front bench seat. Behind him there are junior

A SUMMARY OF MAJOR PARTY VIEWPOINTS

	Conservative	Labour
Basic Philosophy	People are able to get on without government aid. Free enterprise and choice.	Government must be involved to create a fairer and more compassionate society.
Economy	Encourage private enterprise and cut government spending.	Plan for industrial development. Nationalise industries.
Taxation	Few taxes, as low as possible to allow people to spend their own money.	Range of taxes to take money from those who can afford it to help the less well-off.
Wages and Prices	Give top men high wages to reward effort, encourage others to work harder and stop 'brain drain'.	Reduce gap between well-off and less well-off. Tie increases to productivity. Limit all income, and control prices.
Social Services	Charge for services. Encourage private medicine. Increase incentive to work.	Free health and social services. Small charge for some (e.g. prescriptions). Phase out pay beds in NHS hospitals.
Education	Keep selective schools. Keep fee-paying schools.	Encourage comprehensive system. Put fee-paying schools outside state system.
Foreign policy	Sell arms to South Africa. Increase defence spending. Resist threat of communism.	Against South Africa and apartheid. Keep down defence spending.
Government	Keep hereditary peers in House of Lords.	Decrease powers of House of Lords.
Home Affairs	Keen on 'law and order'. Severely limit immigration.	Limit immigration. Keen on good community relations.

ministers and then backbench MPs. On the Speaker's left, the Conservative Party, being the next largest party in the House after this election, occupy the benches of Her Majesty's Opposition. The Shadow Cabinet headed by the Leader of the Opposition occupy the front benches. The task of all Opposition MPs is to examine and criticise the activities of government, while presenting alternative proposals themselves.

The maximum life of a Parliament is five years because convention requires that a General Election must be called at least every five years. The Prime Minister, however, may request the Queen to call an election at any time within the five years. If the government is defeated on a vote of confidence in the House of Commons, convention requires that the government resign in order that another government, commanding a majority in the House, may take over, or, as is more likely, that a general election be held.

The monarch is responsible for the State Opening of Parliament and for the Queen's Speech. In this speech, the government's proposals and intentions for the coming parliamentary session are announced. They are, in fact, drawn up by the Cabinet, and presented to the Queen. After the Queen's Speech, Parliament debates and votes on its content: the first test of the government's majority in the House of Commons.

The following general points about debates in the House should be noted:

Members take turns to speak when called on by the Speaker after 'catching his eye'.

Parliamentary privilege – all MPs enjoy complete freedom of speech within Parliament. This protects their interests and encourages the fullest debate possible.

Unparliamentary language – there is an accepted code that no member of the House will use any form of offensive language to other members. The Speaker applies this rule and anyone refusing to retract such language may be 'named' and

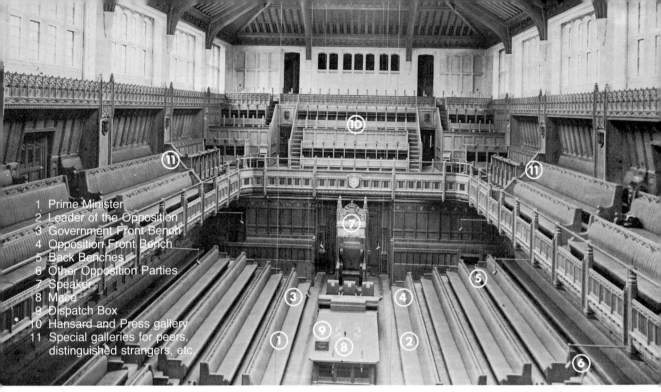

The House of Commons

1 Prime Minister
2 Leader of the Opposition
3 Government Front Bench
4 Opposition Front Bench
5 Back Benches
6 Other Opposition Parties
7 Speaker
8 Mace
9 Dispatch Box
10 Hansard and Press gallery
11 Special galleries for peers, distinguished strangers, etc.

removed from the House.

'Hansard' is the official report of every word that is said in both the House of Lords and the House of Commons.

'Maiden' speech is the first speech in the House by a new member.

The **quorum** for the House of Commons is forty and for the House of Lords is three.

The guillotine is a device used by the government to limit discussion and debate. It sets a timetable for each stage of a bill, at the end of which a vote must be taken.

MAKING A LAW

The main task of Parliament is legislation, i.e. the process of law making. For this process there is an established procedure.

1 **White paper** Most proposed legislation appears as a White Paper, thus giving the government time to take into account comments and criticisms.

2 **The First Reading** All proposed legislation begins as a printed document known as a Bill. The Minister or Private Member responsible for the Bill stands and says, 'Mr Speaker, Sir, a Bill'. This is the formal announcement and presentation of the Bill to the House. MPs then go away and read the Bill.

3 **The Second Reading** allows the House to debate fully the principles and intentions of the Bill. At the end of the debate a vote may be called. At this point the members of Parliament file into the division lobbies to vote yes or no to the principles of the Bill. If the majority vote is against it, the Bill falls. If the majority supports it, the process continues to the next stage.

4 **The Committee Stage** At this point the Bill is examined in great detail and amendments are offered, debated, accepted or rejected. The Committee will normally be a standing committee of the House of Commons. Its make up in terms of political parties will be a reflection of party strengths in the full House. The Scottish Grand Committee, composed of all seventy-one Scottish MPs plus enough other MPs to reflect the party balance in the House, considers all Scottish Bills. Some Bills, e.g. finance bills and constitutional bills, are examined by a Committee of the Whole House of Commons (all MPs are members of this committee).

5 **The Report Stage** allows the House to be informed of the work and findings of the Committee and for any amendments to be moved and voted on by all MPs.

6 **The Third Reading** is the final debate and vote by the House.

The State Opening of Parliament, 1978

significance throughout. The Chief Whip is a member of the Cabinet and, with the help of the Assistant Whips, is responsible for ensuring support for the government by making sure that enough MPs turn up to vote in favour. The Opposition Whips will also be seeking maximum support from their members to oppose the government. Each party issues all its MPs with a daily letter showing the business of the day. Any matter which is underlined once requests attendance. If it is underlined twice, the Whip expects the member's attendance and support. A 'three-line whip' demands attendance and support. There are occasions when three-line whips are disobeyed, e.g. in 1973 sixty-nine Labour MPs supported the Conservative Government's legislation for UK membership of the EEC, but such occurrences are rare and usually result in the offending MPs being disciplined. Normally the Chief Whip will seek an explanation for their voting behaviour and warn the MPs as to their future conduct. An MP who persistently votes against the Party may 'have the whip withdrawn'. This means that he/she cannot attend Parliamentary party meetings and receives no help or information from the party. As a last resort he/she may not be selected to represent the party at the next General Election.

If the Bill is not financial it goes to the House of Lords and through the same process. If it passes through the Lords it will go back to the Commons and then to the Queen for signature (Royal Assent). It will then become an Act of Parliament.

Bills coming before Parliament fall into two main groups:
Government legislation takes up the bulk of Parliamentary time. At all stages the government of the day will try to ensure majority support for its proposals and the whip system is of major

Private Members' Bills are presented on certain Fridays in the session. There is always a ballot and those MPs coming at the top of the list have the greater chance of success.

Most of the remaining time in Parliament is taken up by:
Adjournment debates These normally occur in the last half-hour of the Parliamentary day. By

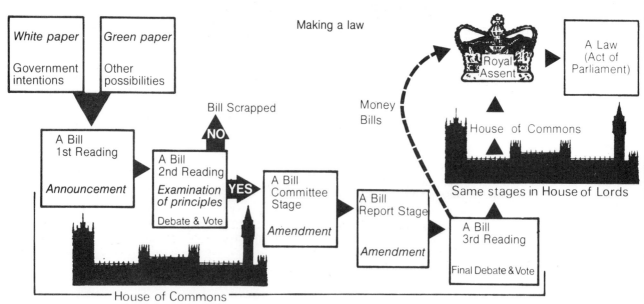

Making a law

tradition a member of the House must propose that the day's business is ended and that the members may adjourn. Any backbencher may move the adjournment and in the process raise topical or urgent matters of concern. No legislation is possible but quite a bit of publicity can be got for individuals or groups. Members ballot for the privilege of raising matters at this time.

Question Time allows members to support, examine and criticise the work of the various ministers. It is an opportunity to demand detailed answers from a minister and to critically examine his performance. All ministers, including the Prime Minister have their share of Question Time. Questions are submitted two or three days in advance to give the minister time to prepare an answer. Often a seemingly innocent question brings an embarrassing supplementary question. If members only want information from a question they will ask for a written reply, but if their aim is to attract publicity to themselves or their cause they will prefer an oral answer.

Opposition time There are twenty-nine 'supply' days each session which allow the Opposition to choose subjects for debate.

A Whip

On Monday, 20th February, 1978, the House will meet at 2.30 p.m.

A Debate will take place on Nationalisation on a Government Motion and an Opposition amendment.

A good attendance throughout this debate is particularly requested. A Division may take place and your attendance at 10 p.m. and until the Prayer is concluded, is particularly requested, unless you have obtained a pair.

On Tuesday, 21st February, 1978, the House will meet at 2.30 p.m.

Conclusion of debate on Nationalisation. The Government may move a Guillotine motion.

There will be most important Divisions and your attendance at 9.30 p.m. is essential.

James Falconer's Private Members' Bill

At the start of his second session in Parliament,

The Whip System

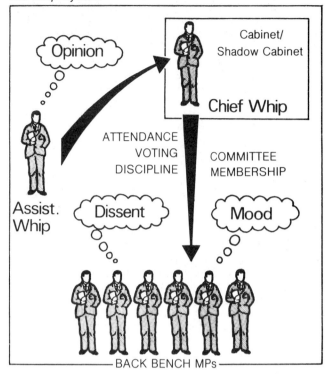

James was lucky enough to have his name drawn in the ballot for Private Members' Bills. This gave him (and another nineteen MPs) the chance to introduce a bill on one of twenty Fridays during the coming parliamentary session.

Since James had no idea what his bill should be about, he asked a few of his more experienced backbench colleagues. 'You don't stand much chance', he was told by some. 'Pick a topic that'll be a vote-catcher. Something to give you a bit of good publicity.' Others said, 'This is your chance to act as an MP should. Make it a worthwhile bill.'

James was a member of the Monday Club but he didn't think their ideas would carry the support of enough MPs.

Then the letters started coming in. People everywhere seemed to know that he had come high up on the ballot and his postbag bulged for weeks with letters from the Society to Prevent This and the Organisation Against That. They even came to his weekly surgeries, all these pressure groups. He did become interested in an idea suggested by the Newtown Working Mothers' Group – that employers should be obliged by law to supply nursery facilities if they employed more than sixty women.

James tried the idea out with a few MPs from all the major parties and got enough encouragement to have a civil servant draft his bill. It had to be worded very carefully to avoid misunderstandings.

The title of the bill became 'Nursery Provision for Children of Nursery-School Age Bill'.

The First Reading of the bill – the formal one – was passed as there were hardly any MPs in the House that Friday – but for the Second Reading the place was packed and James was very nervous as he rose to make his prepared speech. The vote was very close, but on a free vote with no three-line whip, it did get through. Now came the Committee Stage. Unfortunately for James and his bill, several members of the Committee kept coming up with what James thought were trifling complaints. Time was running out. Now he realised why only about twelve per cent of Private Members' Bills are passed compared with ninety-three per cent of government bills. Unless. . . . He went to the Leader of the House to ask if he could use some of the government's time to make sure that the bill got through the Committee Stage on to the Third Reading. He got a friendly letter back, but it said that although many government MPs were keen on the bill it was too sensitive an issue to have this kind of government support, especially since many employers were complaining and saying how this was going to push up prices. The government was concerned to keep price increases down and he was sorry they could not help.

A few days later James was told that as it was near the end of the session, there was no time left in the House for the Report Stage and so his bill would not get through.

Questions

1 Where would Falconer and Brown sit in the House of Commons?   2
2 What is the function of each of the items labelled in the House of Commons photograph on page 11?   6
3 What are the main duties of the Speaker?   3
4 Why does the House of Commons have so many rules?   2
5 Give three possible reasons for the calling of a General Election.   3
6 Describe in detail how an idea can become a law.   10
7 What are the duties of the Opposition during this law-making process?   3
8 What are the duties of the Chief Whip?   5
9 What can the whips do to discipline an MP?   2
10 What opportunities does an MP have to speak in the House?   4
11 What efforts should James Falconer make to have his idea made law in the future?   3
12 Describe in detail who the people in the photograph on page 12 are and what they are doing.   4

THE CABINET

The Prime Minister has appointed Peter Brown Secretary of State for Scotland. This appointment means that Mr Brown will be a member of the Cabinet. In order to understand his work and the work of the Cabinet it is first necessary to understand the principle of the separation of powers.

Within the process of lawmaking and government, there are three different parts:

Separation of Powers

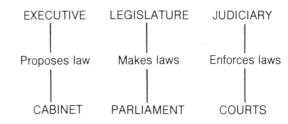

The Executive is the organ for policy decision making. It is the job of the Executive to carry out the government programme. (The Cabinet does not make the law. This is the function of Parliament. It can only suggest what it would like made law.)

The Legislature is the organ responsible for law making. In the British system this is the function of Parliament. In theory, the House of Commons is supreme and controls the Executive and the Judiciary.

The Judiciary has the task of interpreting and implementing the law. It consists of the various levels of judges and is independent both of the Legislature and the Executive in that appointment is for life and is not dependent on any political party.

In the UK, the Executive is the Cabinet, which is composed of the Prime Minister (normally the leader of the majority party in the House of Commons or the leader of the party which can command a majority in the House), the Lord Chancellor and the senior **ministers** of the government. There is no set membership for the Cabinet, the total number of members, usually between twenty and twenty-five, being at the discretion of the Prime Minister. By convention, all members of the Cabinet should be Members of Parliament and are responsible to Parliament.

The Prime Minister is the Chairman of the Cabinet and is responsible for all ministerial appointments. The Cabinet is responsible for all government strategy, decision making and legislative proposals. All members of the Cabinet will take part in discussion, make proposals and participate in any vote. When a Cabinet decision is made, every Cabinet minister is then bound by collective responsibility. This means that he must publicly support the decision even if he was not in agreement. The alternative is that he resign from the Cabinet.

Each minister is responsible to the Prime Minister, the Cabinet and to Parliament for the work and performance of his ministry. Mr Brown, as Secretary of State for Scotland, is responsible, in Scotland, for some work which is done in England and Wales by the Home Secretary and the Ministers of Agriculture, Transport, Social Services and the Environment. He is also responsible for the Scottish educational and legal systems. All government proposals with regard to these areas will be made by Mr Brown, or by his junior ministers. All major ministries have, in addition to the Minister, Junior Ministers of State who assist him in his work and who are normally responsible for particular areas of his remit.

Most ministers are in charge of a particular department, e.g. Energy, the Exchequer or the Home Office, and have their own civil service department. The civil servants are all servants of the Crown. They are public employees who assist ministers to carry out their responsibilities.

The Scottish Office is centred at New St Andrews House, Edinburgh. The top civil servants will be in daily contact with Mr Brown; they will present him with strategy papers and alternatives and will also be responsible for the **administration**

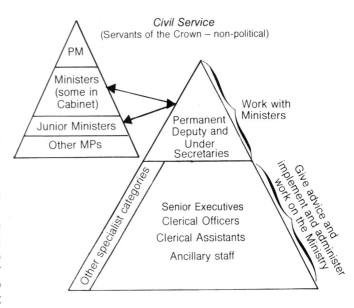

of policies and legislation. Mr Brown is ultimately responsible to Parliament, and he will reply to both oral and written questions put by MPs. He will take day to day decisions on the running of his department and be in charge of general strategy.

The Shadow Cabinet, appointed by the leader of the Opposition, has the task of criticising the work of the Cabinet ministers. A leading member of the Opposition becomes its spokesman on a particular matter, e.g. Energy, and 'shadows' his/her opposite number in the government, being prepared to comment on his/her policies.

The Cabinet

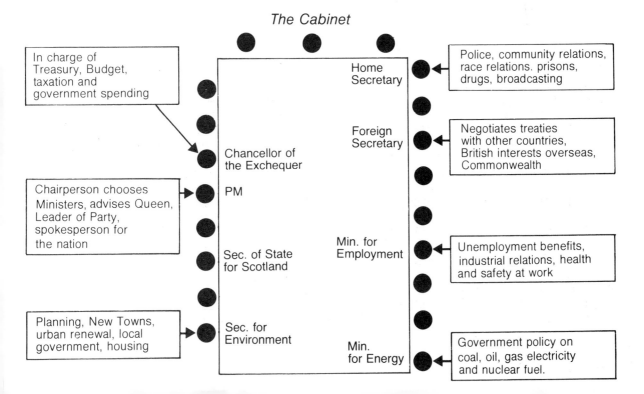

1 List the people involved in each of the following: the Executive, the Legislature, the Judiciary. 6

2 Which Cabinet members would be most involved in a discussion on
   a) police in Scotland;
   b) the building of ships for the navy;
   c) a cut in taxation? 6

3 In what ways does the Civil Service back up the work of Cabinet ministers? 2

4 What are the main duties of each of the following?
   a) Prime Minister;
   b) Shadow Cabinet;
   c) Civil Service. 6

5 What is collective responsibility? Why does the Cabinet have this rule? 3

The Member of Parliament

> **WANTED:** hard working individual, to work in cramped surroundings, on public business. Long hours, night work, no paid overtime. Weekdays at Westminster, weekends at constituency. Working holidays. Share secretary. £12 000 + secretarial allowance, postage and business phone calls. Help with travel. Canteen. Contract for five years maximum. Possible reappointment.

A day in the life of James Falconer MP

8.00	Read selection of newspapers
9.00	Read mail, answer as many as possible
10.00	Meeting with pressure group
11.00	Parliamentary Party meeting
11.30	Backbench 1922 Committee meeting
1.00	Lunch with local newspaper reporter
2.30	Speaker's procession and prayers
2.45	Question Time – put question on constituent's problem – be ready with Supplementary
3.45	Ministerial statement on fishing policy
4.00	Orders of the day – debate on unemployment Two-line whip on divisions
7.00	Possible emergency debate
10.00	Adjournment debate

Aviemore

Dear Peter,
   The kids and I are enjoying our break. What a pity you couldn't join us! You really should try to take a few days off, you know ... all MPs work too hard ... and I don't want you getting ill.
   Before I left, Mrs C from round the corner came by wanting you to do something about her son's grant for university, I gave her a note of when your surgery was, so that you can deal with it. The queue of constituents will be even longer than usual this week.
   You'll really have to get some more notices about the surgery printed – I'm not an information service!
   You'll have heard that James Falconer has had to take on another girl in his estate agent's office. He really can't hope to do two jobs. Perhaps if his business was in London he might manage, but only being here at weekends, and having all the constituency work to do then is almost impossible. Mind you, it could be said that you have two jobs too – being an MP and a Cabinet Minister. I used to think we hardly saw you when you were just an MP. Now the only time we see you is when you're on TV, or behind a mountain of red Dispatch boxes! I think Meg Falconer is getting really fed up with seeing so little of James, she's to deal with everything in the business as well as being mother and father to the kids during the week. It's no wonder there are so many divorces in MPs families.
   We'll be back home in time to meet you off the London plane on Friday afternoon. Let's hope your garden fete doesn't last too long on Saturday ... you really must go to see your mother this weekend ... and please try to leave your papers in London. Sometimes I think I'll have to turn up at your surgery to see you!

Love,
Jean

James Falconer, as a new member of Parliament, is quickly learning the procedure and processes of Parliament. He is already aware of many conflicting pressures on both his time and his loyalties. He recognises four main loyalties:

The national interest must always be in his mind. He is aware of occasions on which some MPs have placed what they see as national interest above all else, e.g. during the EEC debate (1973) and the devolution debate (1977–8).

His party must normally command his support. He accepts that in the UK system most voters vote for parties rather than individuals and that he accepted his party's manifesto throughout his election campaign. The whips remind him of this.

His constituents Both those who voted for and against him must be represented by him, although he insists that he is their **representative**, not their **delegate**.

His conscience will be of major importance, especially in matters of social legislation where he will normally have a free vote, e.g. issues such as capital punishment, abortion and euthanasia.

Clearly there will be occasions when his loyalties will conflict. If there is a matter of conscience which will prevent him supporting his party he will inform the Chief Whip. Usually such an exercise of conscience will be accepted, but if it happens

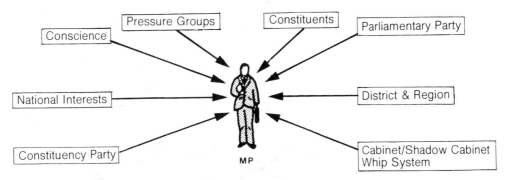

regularly then the party and the whip system will bring pressure to bear and may, as a last resort, discipline him.

His parliamentary day starts at 2.30 p.m., Monday to Thursday, and earlier on a Friday. There is no set time for the end of the parliamentary day and debates have been known to last all night. Before 2.30 he has to sort out his mail, arrange replies where necessary, prepare his work for the day, research the issues due to be raised in the House, prepare any written or oral questions he may wish to ask, and be in contact with his parliamentary colleagues and the whips. From 2.30 onwards he will be in Parliament, which starts with the Speaker's procession and prayers. He may attend debates or be working outside the Chamber but available to vote in any division of the House, when he hears the Division Bell. As a Scottish member of Parliament he attends the Scottish Grand Committee which deals with the committee stage of all Scottish bills. He also has to prepare his maiden speech in the House. Traditionally it should be of modest length and non-controversial but it will be a valuable experience for future debates.

In addition to his parliamentary duties, James Falconer also has to attend to his constituency. As an MP elected from a highly marginal constituency, he must be very attentive to the needs and demands of his constituency. Every Friday during the parliamentary session he travels home to his Newtown constituency. He meets his election agent and discusses the business of the weekend. He will hold his 'surgery' on Saturday in the town hall. The surgery is advertised in the local paper and gives his constituents the opportunity to raise matters of concern to them personally. The matters they raise may require Mr Falconer to contact a local authority, or a national body, such as the Vehicle Licensing Centre, on their behalf. It may, however, be a subject which he will wish to

raise in the House of Commons at Question Time.

As the local MP he is also occupied most weekends in political, social and charitable engagements. These might include party meetings, talks, party and town social events, the opening of fêtes, and interviews with the local press and television. This keeps him in the public eye and raises his popularity. On Sunday night he returns to London for another parliamentary week.

Questions

1 What things would encourage you to apply for the job of MP? What would put you off?   6
2 What can an MP do to make his/her day less busy?   2
3 Write a letter from Peter to his wife Jean answering some of the points raised.   5
4 Why are each of the pressures on MPs important to them? Give examples.   6
5 What part does a surgery play in democracy?   2

Issues

In studying Parliament and government we must look at major issues which arise. In these pages we look at several matters of national and constitutional importance.

Executive versus Legislature

In theory the elected House of Commons is supreme. In practice, the system has developed in such a way that the Executive (Cabinet) increasingly dominates the Legislature (Commons). Cabinet business demands most of Parliament's time and the statistics show that its legislative success is much greater than that of the ordinary MP. Even in the 19th century, Disraeli could demand of his supporters, 'Damn your principles, sir, stick to your party!' and it is undoubtedly true that most members of the Commons are loyal to and support their party.

Why is it that Mr Brown and his Cabinet colleagues can expect support? Why will Mr Falconer be inclined to support his party on most occasions?

The reasons lie in an electoral system that has consistently produced two major political parties in terms of parliamentary voting strength. The two-party system led to a strong party discipline expressed in the whip system. The ordinary MP is also faced with the following pressures:

a) The British electorate tend to vote for a party rather than an individual, so the individual's parliamentary career will depend, at least in part, on his/her party and constituency continuing to accept him/her as their representative and candidate.
b) If the Member of Parliament is a member of the Government, he/she knows that defeat on a vote of confidence could mean a General Election which his/her party might lose.
c) The two-party system heightens party conflict and to vote against his/her party or even to abstain may be interpreted as giving support to the Opposition.
d) If the matter at issue was contained in his/her party's election manifesto, he/she will be expected to give his/her support and his/her vote.

e) The MP who is keen to achieve promotion knows that one yardstick will be his/her loyalty to the party and its legislative proposals.

MPs, however, are not totally without influence. At parliamentary party meetings they will have an opportunity to air their points of view, but if they are minority ones they will be expected to accept the majority view. They can also inform the whips of any dissatisfaction. In 1969, a large group of Labour MPs used this method to end any possibility of the Labour Government introducing **industrial relations** legislation, which they saw as being against the interests of trade unions, based on the document 'In Place of Strife'. As a last resort, the MP can abstain or vote against any proposal. The fact that this is a rare occurrence is a demonstration of the power of the Executive.

Reform of the House of Lords

The House of Lords is the other house in Parliament. It has over 1000 members, none of whom are elected. Its members include hereditary peers, life peers, law lords, archbishops (of York and Canterbury) and twenty-four bishops of the Church of England. Although the importance of the Lords has decreased in the 20th century, it still has two important functions. It debates bills (except Money Bills), especially those parts which may have been hurried through the House of Commons. Occasionally it introduces bills. The Lords can vote against a bill but cannot delay its passage for more than a year.

Throughout this century, there has been continuing criticism of the membership and role of the House of Lords. Its opponents argue that as a non-elected chamber it should not have the power to restrict the activities of an elected House of Commons. It is also criticised for its inbuilt Conservative bias and for the fact that many of its members qualify for membership by the hereditary principle. It has been said to be an institution 'kept alive by absenteeism', thus suggesting that poor attendance reduced its active role. In 1977, however, the Lords did block a Labour Government bill to nationalise the shipbuilding and ship repairing industries and this renewed demands for its reform or abolition. In 1978, the House of Lords made over a hundred amendments to the Devolution Bill, but most of these were rejected by the House of Commons when the Bill was returned to them.

Previous reforms

The 1911 and 1949 Parliament Acts, introduced by a Liberal and Labour Government respectively, severely limited the blocking powers of the Lords, by limiting their power to delay legislation to a year, after which the same bill must be passed. In 1958, the Conservative Government introduced the Life Peerages Act which allowed for the appointment of citizens who had made an important contribution to society, as life peers. The 1963 Peerages Act allowed hereditary peers to disclaim their peerage and stand for election to the House of Commons (Sir Alec Douglas-Home, Quintin Hogg and Anthony Wedgwood Benn were all originally hereditary peers). Many commentators claim, however, that further changes are necessary. In considering several possible changes, it is important to note the possible consequences.

Further reforms

Abolition This would remove the House of Lords and produce a one-chamber system. It would also increase the work of the Commons and end the opportunity for a second look at a bill, which could mean even greater Executive dominance.

The 1969 Wilson proposals that hereditary peers be non-voting members and that there be 230 voting peers (105 government, 80 main opposi-

tion, 15 other parties and 30 cross-benchers). In future, hereditary titles should not carry membership of the Lords. These proposals, however, mean another non-elected chamber responsible only to themselves and possibly appointed by the Prime Minister and the Executive.

An Elected House, elected at the same time as the House of Commons would at least be responsible to the electorate. But, if both Houses were elected by the simple majority system they would tend to be a reflection of each other, and if a different voting system were used for the second chamber (e.g. proportional representation) then there would be the danger of conflict between the Houses.

An Elected House, elected at a different time from the Commons (as in the USA) has been proposed. This, however, might lead to a government having no majority in the second House and being unable to govern.

Clearly the present House of Lords is an anachronism in a democratic society but the best method to reform it is not so clear.

The Monarchy

The monarch, at present Queen Elizabeth the Second, has many **constitutional** powers, as shown in the diagram. In practice, the monarch does not exercise most of these powers but must, under the constitution, act on the advice of government ministers. Her main role today is a symbolic one which can unite the nation and the

The role of the monarch

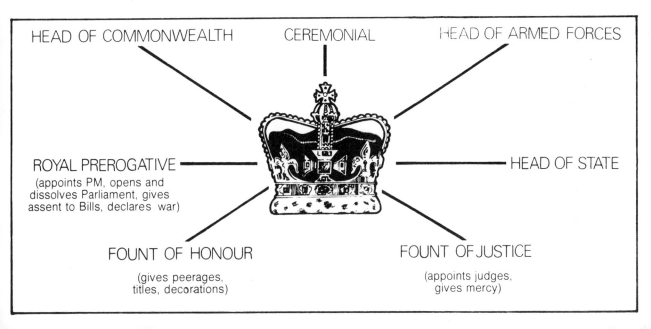

HEAD OF COMMONWEALTH   CEREMONIAL   HEAD OF ARMED FORCES

ROYAL PREROGATIVE
(appoints PM, opens and dissolves Parliament, gives assent to Bills, declares war)

HEAD OF STATE

FOUNT OF HONOUR
(gives peerages, titles, decorations)

FOUNT OF JUSTICE
(appoints judges, gives mercy)

Commonwealth. To this end she, and other members of the Royal Family, are often called upon to undertake ceremonial duties, such as greeting important visitors and recognising the completion of important projects.

However, there is occasional criticism of the monarchy as an institution. Some people resent the fact that in Britain, unlike many other countries, the Head of State is an inherited rather than an elected office. The monarch is said to represent an upper-class elite which divides rather than unites the nation. The cost of supporting the monarch, royal family and other associates is also a common criticism. The cost of the royal yacht, the Queen's Flight, the upkeep of the royal palaces and other conspicuous examples of wealth, whether inherited or paid for by Parliament, amounts to millions of pounds.

It seems likely however, especially since the highly successful Jubilee Year, that as long as a British monarch does not attempt to enforce his or her theoretical power over government ministers, the widespread popularity of and interest in the royal family will continue. The monarch reigns but does not rule, and this makes a republican Britain unlikely.

Government and the Economy

Over the years, governments have taken more and more responsibility for providing services for the nation. For centuries it was accepted that the defence of the nation could best be organised by a central administration rather than by individuals or small groups. Other services followed.

Government intervention on a large scale was accepted after 1945, with the introduction of the Welfare State to provide **environmental** and social services. To do so it was necessary to raise **revenue** from a variety of sources. As with an individual or family budget, it is important that, over a period of time, the nation does not spend more than its income. If the nation's budget remains 'in the red' (deficit), the nation will become **bankrupt**. If it balances its budget, or is 'in the black' (surplus), the nation prospers.

THE BUDGET

Traditionally the government of the day introduces one Budget around April of each year. In recent years, however, there have been a number of 'mini' budgets in addition to the normal April one. This is partly due to prolonged economic difficulties which require adjustments to the economic system more than once a year, and partly to increased government involvement in the economy.

Any Budget is normally a statement of the Government's policy on money and **taxation** (monetary and fiscal policy). Basically it is concerned with income (revenue) and expenditure. Therefore, a Budget will give details of changes in taxation (direct and indirect), National Insurance contributions (both employers and employees) and the programme of Government spending within each of the ministries. Each Budget should have an overall economic and financial plan.

There is also a social side to the Budget. A Chancellor of the Exchequer can allocate more money to any group in society, such as old age pensioners or the unemployed. He can announce measures designed to lessen unemployment or

Public expenditure 1976–7

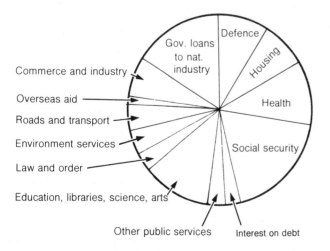

Government income 1976–7

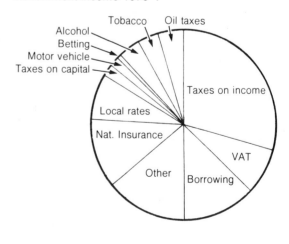

inflation. He can even discourage smoking, drinking, or gambling (or any other vice!) by increasing the tax or duty on it.

When the Budget is presented to the House of Commons by the Chancellor of the Exchequer, the normal procedure is followed. At the Committee Stage, it is a Committee of the Whole House which examines the Budget. Since the Budget is part of the Government's financial role, the House of Lords cannot block, hinder or defeat it.

Questions

1 In what ways has the Cabinet become more powerful than the Commons?	4
2 What powers does an MP still have?	2
3 What are the arguments for and against the retention of the House of Lords?	4
4 In what ways might the House of Lords be reformed?	4
5 Give the arguments for and against keeping the monarchy in its present form.	6
6 Why is a Budget necessary at least once a year?	4
7 What items are likely to be mentioned in a Budget?	3
8 Where does the Government get most of its money from?	2
9 What does the Government spend most of its money on?	2
10 What happens on Budget day?	3

Nationalism and Devolution

Since the late 1960s the Scottish and Welsh Nationalists have emerged as a significant political force. In the same period the two major parties have moved towards a commitment to some form of devolved government for Scotland and Wales. Three Welsh Nationalist and eleven Scottish Nationalist MPs were elected in October, 1974. The main reasons for the rise of the Scottish Nationalists include:

From an historical perspective the Union of the Crowns (1707) is fairly recent and there always has been some resistance to it in various areas of Scottish political life.
The changed style of the SNP, especially the departure from a 'kilt and haggis' image.
A growing disenchantment with centralised government.
The SNP appeared to some voters as an alternative in a two-party system where few voters cross over from Labour to Conservative or vice versa.
An increasing criticism of the performance of Labour and Conservative governments with regard to their attitude to Scotland, e.g. money allocation. The fact that no British government, of whatever party, can fully satisfy the economic, industrial and social needs of different regions, particularly within a declining economy.
The discovery of North Sea Oil gave greater credibility to SNP economic arguments and forecasts, especially when viewed alongside Scotland's problems of **declining** traditional industries, persistently high rates of unemployment and increasing **multiple deprivation** in the cities.
The example of other nations achieving their **independence** (decolonisation) and the success of small nations such as Norway.
People in Scotland have retained a sense of national and cultural identity.

It is interesting to note, however, that opinion polls have consistently shown that the majority of Scots, even SNP voters, do not support total separation and independence. Nevertheless the opinion polls also demonstrate that the voting patterns in Scotland have changed: Labour, Conservative and SNP at times receiving almost equal support.

THE SCOTTISH ASSEMBLY

The Kilbrandon Commission's suggestion in 1973 of **devolution** for Scotland and Wales was taken up by the Labour government. At the second attempt a bill went through all stages in Parliament to become the Scotland Act, 1978.

The main proposals were that the Assembly, to be set up in Edinburgh, would have 150 members and choose a First Secretary. It would advise the Secretary of State for Scotland on the appointment of a ministerial team called the 'Scottish Secretaries'. It would have control of **services** totalling over £2500 million a year. It would have power to make new laws for Scotland in the areas it controls: health; social work; care of the elderly, children and handicapped; schools and further education, except the universities; housing; planning; local government; transport; criminal law; civil law; the arts; fresh water fisheries and crofting; tourism; the courts; licensing laws; fire services; summer time; shop hours; registration of births, marriages and deaths. The Assembly would have a staff of about 250, a civil service of another

750, with headquarters in the old Royal High School, Edinburgh.

The Act also said that a **referendum** should be held to consult the Scottish people but a controversial clause said that forty per cent of those eligible to vote in the referendum on the Scotland Act would have to vote 'Yes', and if not, Parliament would have a further opportunity to repeal the Act. (A slightly different set of proposals were put to the Welsh people.)

The View of the Major Parties

In the run-up to the referendum on 1 March, 1979, the views of the main parties were:

Labour: The party in Scotland was behind the Act, as it fulfilled the promise made in the 1974 manifesto.
Conservative: Campaigned for a 'No' vote in the Referendum, saying that the Act had been passed too hurriedly, that it meant more government rather than better government, and that it might lead to the break-up of the United Kingdom.
SNP: Supported the Act as a stepping stone to independence, though criticised the lack of revenue-raising powers.
Liberals: Supported the Act, though would have preferred the Assembly to have more power as part of a federal system of government for the whole of Britain.

Within each party there was a minority which disagreed with the 'party line' and some actively campaigned against the view of the party.

The Referendum Result

	% Yes	% No
Borders	26.7	39.7
Central	36.1	29.9
Dumfries and Galloway	25.8	38.3
Fife	35.1	30.3
Grampian	27.6	29.5
Highland	33.0	31.7
Lothian	33.0	32.9
Orkney	15.1	39.0
Shetland	13.6	36.7
Strathclyde	33.7	28.7
Tayside	31.2	31.8
Western Isles	27.8	22.1
Total	32.5	30.4

These figures are percentages of those shown on the electoral register. (In Wales, the vote was 11.8% Yes, 46.5% No.)

As the table shows, although the 'Yes' vote won a narrow victory, it did not reach the required forty per cent.

This annoyed the supporters of the 'Yes' campaign, particularly the SNP, who claimed that a majority of those who voted should be enough to introduce a Scottish Assembly. However, the election of a Conservative Government in 1979 should lead to a repeal of the Scotland Act and the offer of all-party talks.

The European Dimension

In 1973, the Conservative Government led Britain into the European Community. In 1975, the new Labour Government organised a referendum and the majority of voters elected to remain in the EEC. As a member of the EEC, Britain is now involved in and affected by the major bodies who run the community.

These are a) The Council of Ministers
b) The European Commission
c) The European Parliament

THE COUNCIL OF MINISTERS

Each member government sends a minister to the Council. Normally it is the Foreign Minister but, for particular topics, the minister most directly concerned is sent, e.g. the Minister of Agriculture or the Chancellor of the Exchequer. The council is a decision-making body. If there is a difference of opinion, a vote is taken, each member state having a certain number of votes:

Britain	10	Belgium	5
France	10	Netherlands	5
Italy	10	Denmark	3
W. Germany	10	Eire	3
Luxemburg	2		

From the total number of fifty-eight, forty-one votes are necessary to reach a decision. However, any member state can veto any proposal.

THE EUROPEAN COMMISSION

The Commission is made up of thirteen commissioners, each appointed by national governments but not a member of that government. Each commissioner is in charge of one area of the Community's responsibility, e.g. transport or agriculture. Their main task is to establish policy, which is then sent to the European Parliament and then to the Council of Ministers. The commissioners also apply the rules of the Community.

THE EUROPEAN PARLIAMENT

A total of 198 delegates are sent to the Parliament. Each is already a member of his own national parliament. The 198 seats are allocated as follows:

France	36	Belgium	14
Italy	36	Netherlands	14
W. Germany	36	Denmark	10
Britain	36	Eire	10
Luxemburg	6		

Britain is also affected by the Court of Justice, made up of lawyers from each member country and any person or organisation can refer to the Court any matter which they consider to be against the rules of the EEC or the Treaty of Rome.

As a member of the EEC, Britain accepts the rules of the Community. Our government, therefore, is tied to the principle of common policies in, for example, transport, agriculture and fisheries, taxation, external **trade**, custom's duties and tariffs, energy and free movement of labour.

Opponents of Britain's membership of the European Community are concerned that Britain is now bound by the rules and regulations of the Community and that decisions made in Brussels can be binding on Britain. They consider that our sovereignty, or freedom to run our own affairs, is restricted. Supporters of membership would probably concede that there have been some constraints on Britain's freedom but point out that they are minor, that Parliament voted to join the Community and accept its structure, and that the benefits of membership more than make up for the losses in sovereignty.

Until 1979 only nominated MPs of the UK Parliament attended the European Parliament. The first European Parliament elections were held in 1979 and from them MPs were elected directly to the European Parliament.

Britain will have eighty-one members representing eighty-one constituencies. It is hoped that direct election will lead to a more powerful European Parliament and it is seen by some as the first stage towards greater political **integration** of all the countries in the Community.

Questions

1 Why has the popularity of nationalism increased in recent years?   4
2 Do you think the proposals for the Scottish Assembly go far enough?   3
3 What do the four main parties think of devolution?   8
4 What are the duties of each of the following: Council of Ministers, European Commission, European Parliament?   6
5 What effect has EEC membership had on British government?   3
6 'There is too much democracy in Britain.' Give arguments for and against this statement.   6

Local Government (Scotland)

Table 3   Scottish Regions

Region	Population (1971)	Population (1976)
Borders	98 782	99 917
Central	263 184	270 056
Dumfries and Galloway	143 530	143 585
Fife	328 028	338 734
Grampian	437 231	453 829
Highland	175 449	186 460
Islands authorities	65 422	66 403
Lothian	742 257	755 293
Strathclyde	2 578 314	2 488 643
Tayside	396 766	402 180

In addition to Central Government, Scotland has a system of local government. Local government is, in fact, the oldest form of government, having existed long before central government or national government.

We have local government for several reasons:

to identify locally, the needs and problems of the individual citizen;
to offer citizens the opportunity to participate in the business of government;
to keep a check on central government.

The functions of local government are of two main types:

Those involving responsibility for matters of local concern and importance.
Those involving the administration of services entrusted to local authorities by central government.

Local authorities, although elected democratically, do not determine their own power or responsibilities. These are laid down by Act of Parliament.

Structure

In 1975, a new structure of local government was introduced, based on the Wheatley Report (1969) and on a Government White Paper introduced in 1971. Before 1975, there were five types of Scottish local authority based on the Local Government (Scotland) Act 1929. They were: Cities – 4; Large Burghs – 21; Small Burghs – 176; Counties – 33; Districts – 196.

The Wheatley Report stated that 'something is seriously wrong with local government in Scotland', and concluded that the basic problem was one of structure. The main criticisms were:

That there were too many authorities and levels of authority.
That the allocation of functions was arbitrary, and that these functions could be carried out more efficiently by a different type of authority.
That the authorities were over-dependent on central government.
That they were inefficient.
That the public was apathetic, e.g. in 1967, as many as sixty-three seats were uncontested and fifty-three per cent of the electorate did not vote.

The Report sought four main aims for the new authorities:
Power – local government should have greater responsibilities and to be less dependent on central government.
Effectiveness – every local government service should operate on a scale which would allow high standards, good value for money and greater efficiency.
Local democracy – locally elected bodies should be genuinely in charge of the local situation and responsible to the local electorate.
Local involvement – people should be brought into the process of reaching decisions.

THE NEW STRUCTURE

In 1975 a new two-tier system (with special provision for the Islands and the addition of Community Councils) was introduced. Scotland was divided into nine Regions, which were the first tier of the new structure. Each Region was sub-divided into Districts. In total there are fifty-three District Councils. (There are also three multi-purpose Island Authorities outwith the two-tier system. These are in Orkney, Shetland and the Western Isles.) The number of Districts per Region are:

Region	District
Borders	4
Central	3
Dumfries and Galloway	4
Fife	3
Grampian	5
Highland	8
Lothian	4
Strathclyde	19
Tayside	3

The overall plan is that the functions of local government can best be allocated to one of two levels of authority. The District is clearly more concerned with local matters, while the Region is responsible for services requiring planning and administration over a larger geographical area. Some services are shared jointly by the two tiers, e.g. museums and galleries, and recreation. The decision to have multi-purpose Island Authorities was a recognition of their distinct geographic and social character.

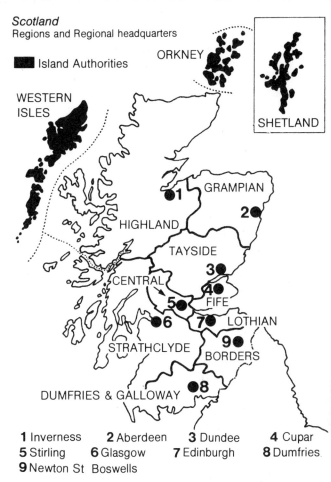

Scotland
Regions and Regional headquarters

■ Island Authorities

1 Inverness **2** Aberdeen **3** Dundee **4** Cupar
5 Stirling **6** Glasgow **7** Edinburgh **8** Dumfries
9 Newton St Boswells

Strathclyde Region

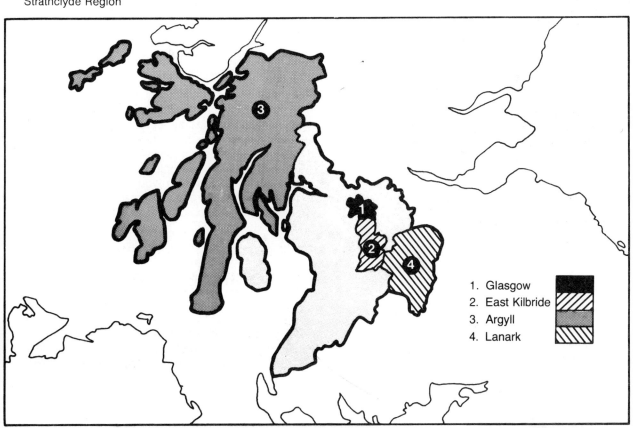

1. Glasgow
2. East Kilbride
3. Argyll
4. Lanark

In addition to the two main tiers, Community Councils were set up. It was decided that any community could choose to form an elected Community Council. It would have no statutory powers, but would be a vehicle for expressing local views and taking local action. The overall responsibility for the setting up of such Councils with codes of procedure and arrangements for elections is that of the Island or District Authorities. These Community Councils may raise funds, and receive special project grants. They can also expect help – money, staff and facilities – from Regional, Island or District Councils.

One major aim of the re-structuring was to relax central government control over local authorities. By the Act of 1973, the Secretary of State for Scotland can decide that powers which refer to local authorities, given to central government by earlier legislation, can be withdrawn, thus giving the new authorities a greater control over their own affairs. Some relaxation of central government control has already taken place:

Transport Formerly central government had control over passenger transport authorities. This has been withdrawn and as a result, bodies such as the Greater Glasgow Passenger Transport Executive are no longer responsible to central government.

Local Authority borrowing Still controlled by central government but efforts have been made to abolish some aspects of this control or at least to make it more flexible and allow the local authority a wider scope for borrowing and therefore greater independence. A local authority can also operate a lottery scheme, provided it is within the law, without seeking special permission from Parliament.

Many critics argue that to achieve a real degree of independence of local authorities from central government requires a change in the financial structure of local authorities.

Finance

Despite the major reforms which have taken place, the financial structure has not enjoyed such dramatic changes. Local authority sources of finance remain:

a) Current income, which includes trading income, rents, and **interest**. This includes income from housing, transport and entertainment.

b) Rates – a tax paid to the authority on all buildings within its boundaries. Every building, house, shop, cinema and factory has a rateable value (RV). The RV on property depends on several factors, e.g. size and type of property and location. This system allocates a greater rateable value to larger houses than to smaller ones.

The rates are calculated as follows: the authority determines the total RV of all property in its area. It also calculates its total **expenditure** for the year. It subtracts the amount it will receive from central government. The amount left is divided by the total RV and the answer is the rate for every pound of RV. For example:

Total expenditure   £69 851 675
Government grant –   28 431 710

Amount to be borne
by rates   41 419 965

$$\therefore \text{Rate} = \frac{41\ 419\ 965}{30\ 700\ 000\ (RV)} = 1.40$$

Therefore a house with a rateable value of £75 will pay

$$£(75 \times 1.4) = £105$$

These rates are calculated by both the Regional and District authorities. Therefore the rates which a property owner pays are made up of both a Regional and a District rate.

c) Exchequer **grants** are the money received from central government. This includes a 'Rate Support Grant' to keep rates as low as possible.

d) Borrowing – people can .invest in a local authority to get a rate of interest just as they can invest in a public company.

Many commentators believe that the rates system is the area most in need of reform. As it stands, a household, consisting of a couple with five children and only the father working, pays the same rates as another family in the same type and size of house with a couple, both earning, and five children, three of whom work, and live at home. However, alternatives such as a local income tax or a local sales tax would be difficult to introduce and to operate.

Criticisms and Problems

Although reform is fairly recent there are already serious criticisms levelled at the new system. It should be noted, however, before examining some criticisms, that problems which existed

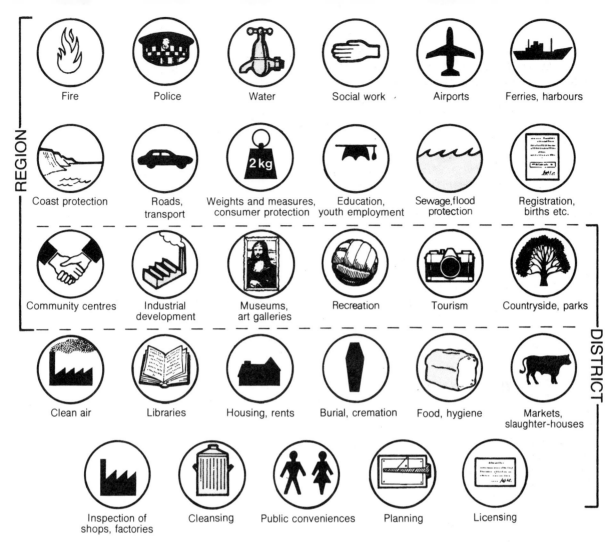

Functions of Local Authorities

before the reform cannot be blamed on the new authorities.

One criticism is that the new structure still depends on central government and relies on an inefficient financial structure. Another is that the Regions are too big and too impersonal. While conceding that some matters can be most efficiently planned on a large scale, the critics insist that regionalisation is yet another example of the separation of the electorate from important governmental decisions. They point out that, for example, Strathclyde extends from Argyll to Kyle and Carrick, and includes old cities, new towns and agricultural areas, and contains almost a half of Scotland's population, while Highland Region covers a huge area with very few people.

A new issue arose with the possibility of a Scottish Assembly. If this form of devolved Scottish government were to be established there could be several problems:

A growing sense of overgovernment among the electorate, with authorities ranging from the District to European Parliament and a consequent danger of apathy and confusion.

The possibility that a Scottish Assembly might not wish to accept the continuance of large regional authorities.

A Scottish Assembly might wish to have control over certain services which are at present in the hands of the Region.

It is clear that a new system of local government was necessary in the interests of greater efficiency, participation and a lessening dependence on central government. The number of councils and councillors have been greatly reduced and services have been allocated on a more sensible basis. Nevertheless the future of the new structure remains in doubt.

Community Views Rejected

Last night at a stormy meeting of the Glenforth District Housing Committee, Councillor Cunningham refused to accept the proposals of the Glenforth Central Community Council for the development of twenty houses for single people on vacant land, and instead accepted the recommendation of Councillor Jones that no action should be taken until the Planning and Development Committee and the Finance Committee of the Regional Council meet next month.

Fred Johnston, Chairman of the Central Community Council said today, 'They are only interested in more expenses, that lot. Always delaying decisions saying they need approval from the Region or Government. Piece of nonsense. Last month it was education they said they couldn't touch – Region's business. I know for a fact they are responsible for housing – but now they say that money comes from the Region and its all part of the Region's plan. Where does the ordinary working man fit into all this that's what I want to know.'

Councillor Cunningham, on his way to work today, explained that though the District has charge of certain services, the Regional Council has overall control of what happens within the whole region. He denied charges of holding meetings to make money – 'We get a flat rate attendance allowance and travelling expenses. Oh, and something for food. Quote me on that!'

Questions

1. List the nine regions in order of geographical size and in order of population size. What can you say about the difference between the two lists?   8
2. Which region is losing people? What effect does this have on local government?   2
3. Why do we have local government?   2
4. What was wrong with the old system of local government?   3
5. In what ways are the new authorities an improvement on the old?   4
6. What special problems do these three regions have:
   Strathclyde; Fife; Highland?   6
7. What are the duties of a Community Council?   2
8. Describe the different sources of local government revenue. What other ways might there be of raising money?   4
9. In what ways would a Scottish Assembly affect local government?   2
10. To which councillor (Regional or District) would you go if you wished to complain about: pollution of the air, a hole in a road, dirty water, housing, dustmen, schools, noise from a pub, an OAP in need of help?   4
11. What problems does Glenforth Community Council have?   2

The Mass Media

In any society the mass **media** play a significant and influential role. They have been described as the 'Fourth Estate' after the Houses of Lords and Commons, the People and the Church. Press radio and television share similar functions:

To *inform* on news ranging from the local to international.

To *educate* by providing information in a structured manner. In addition, both radio and TV provide school and university education programmes.

To *entertain.* Newspapers entertain by providing articles, features and cartoons. Radio and TV have an obligation to provide a balanced programme of entertainment, including drama, films and the arts.

To *persuade* and *influence.* The most obvious attempt to influence is through advertising. Less obviously, each newspaper has a political standpoint which it wishes to convey to the reader. This editorial slant will affect its editorials, its emphasis and its approach to significant political, social and economic events. Few editors deliberately wish to deceive their readers but it is possible for the same story to appear differently in two different newspapers. An article can appear on the front page of one paper with a banner headline, and at the bottom of an inside page in another. Even photographs can be slanted: they can show a politician looking honest or sly.

By Acts of Parliament, television and radio are supposed to ensure that a proper balance of views is expressed. Therefore, although individuals and political parties can express political views through these mediums, these will be balanced by the views of others. This applies not only to party political broadcasts but also to documentaries, discussion programmes, etc.

Newspapers
PRESENTATION OF NEWS

Since the main aim of a newspaper is to sell as many papers as possible, the way it presents its news must be attractive to its readers. Newspaper owners seem to aim their newspapers at one of two different types of reader: one who wants a lot of information presented in a straightforward way, and who is interested in politics, **industry** and business (the 'quality' paper); and one who wants the most important bits of information but also wants a lot of entertainment (the 'popular' paper). Since some people buy both types of paper there is no such thing as a typical 'quality' reader or a typical 'popular' reader.

Characteristic	Quality	Popular
Size	Broadsheet	Tabloid
Photographs	Few	Many
News stories	Politics, business, foreign affairs, sport	Mainly human interest but also most important events
Language	Often difficult to read	Simple, short sentences, easy to read
Headlines	Long, explanatory	Short, snappy
Background articles	Informative on important issues	'Secret confessions', sometimes simplified explanation of Budget, etc.
Magazine elements	Reviews of theatre, books, films, fashion, crosswords	Crosswords, pin-ups, pop stars, footballers, gossipy woman's page, competitions

Every quality newspaper will not have the same characteristics and every popular newspaper will not be identical. Each has its own style.

Local MP promises action for working mothers

James Falconer made an important speech yesterday when he opened St Jude's Garden Fête, which may give a hint as to the subject he will choose for his Private Members' Bill later this session. He commented on the increasing number of nursery places needed in the constituency because of the recently opened factories employing women. He said, 'In this age of equality, I believe it to be the right of every woman to go out to work. Without sufficient nursery places in the area, the married women in this constituency are at a disadvantage. I intend to do everything in my power to make it illegal for any authority to have fewer nursery places than the number of nursery school-age children in its area.'

Mr Falconer and his wife spent the afternoon at the fête, which was held in aid of churches in West Africa, a cause which Mrs Falconer has worked for in the past.

Jimmy's Sweet Moment

Handsome local MP, James Falconer, brought the house down yesterday when he kissed Betty McFadden (65), winner of the garden fête's sweet-making competition. Said Betty, a grandmother of four, 'He doesn't need any of my sweets, he's sweet enough already.'

After his speech opening the fête, James and his beautiful young wife, who wore a turquoise silk dress and matching feather hat spent the afternoon touring the stalls with the Rev. Williamson, an old schoolfriend of Mr Falconer.

During his visit Mr Falconer spoke to stallholders many of whom are customers of his estate agency in the town.

As they left, Mrs Falconer was presented with a bouquet of red roses by Patricia Williamson (5), daughter of the Rev. Williamson.

The type of advertising appearing in each newspaper also varies. An advertiser is aiming for a particular market and therefore a particular type of newspaper reader: a supermarket advert is more likely to appear in a popular paper read by housewives and an advert for an airline company in a quality paper read by business people.

As well as grouping newspapers as popular or quality, there are daily or weekly papers; morning or evening newspapers; local, provincial or national papers.

ORGANISATION

The organisation of a newspaper can be divided into three main phases:

Collection Written news reports are presented by staff reporters, freelance reporters, foreign correspondents, etc. Articles and news items are also written up from stories sent in by news agencies such as Reuters, Press Association and Extel. Added to this is information on the weather, TV and radio programmes, classified advertisements as well as feature articles and special interest pages.

Visual material – photographs, cartoons and other graphics have also to be collected.

Editing and presentation Major newspapers have editors in charge of news, foreign affairs, sport, features, etc. Their task is to decide on the final length of reports and to check on their accuracy. Sub-editors write up received stories to the correct length.

The Editor-in-Chief decides on the general attitude of the newspaper, and his/her policy will be reflected in the contents of the paper. One of his/her tasks is to write the editorial, where the view of the newspaper on a major news item is given. He/she also takes decisions on the final layout of the paper, especially the front page.

Production and distribution All articles are typeset, sometimes using a computer, and printed. They are then distributed to newspaper sellers and newsagents.

OWNERSHIP

Most national newspapers are owned by a few large publishing groups, most of which also have interests in other branches of the media, such as commercial television, commercial radio and magazines. Some of these groups are, in turn, owned by larger organisations.

Table 4 National newspapers

Owner	Newspaper	Circulation (1978)
Reed International	Daily Mirror	3 778 000
	Sunday People	3 853 000
	Sunday Mirror	3 832 000
Trafalgar House Ltd	Daily Express	2 400 000
	Sunday Express	3 242 000
News International Ltd	The Sun	3 930 000
	News of the World	4 934 000
Thomson Organisation Ltd	The Times	293 000
	The Sunday Times	1 409 000
Daily Telegraph Ltd	Daily Telegraph	1 344 000
	Sunday Telegraph	844 000
Guardian and Manchester Evening News Ltd.	The Guardian	273 000
Atlantic Richfield Co. & Observer Trust	The Observer	688 000

The fewer newspapers there are, the greater chance of only a few points of view being available. Where there is a danger of a group having a **monopoly** in the media, because of takeover or bankruptcy, the matter can be referred to the Monopolies and Mergers Commission. This includes cases where newspaper owners may have an interest in owning **commercial** television and/or radio stations. In this way it is hoped that a wide range of opinions will be available to the public.

Table 5 Scottish newspapers

Owner	Newspaper	Circulation (1978)
Lonrho (Scottish Universal Newspapers)	Glasgow Herald	118 000
Thomson Organisation Ltd	Scotsman	92 000
	Aberdeen Press and Journal	115 000
Reed International	Daily Record	722 000
	Sunday Mail	773 000
D C Thompson	Dundee Courier and Advertiser	133 710
	Sunday Post	n.a. but over 1 million

Table 6 Scottish evening papers

Owner	Newspaper	Circulation
Lonrho	Evening Times (Glasgow)	219 000
Thomson Organisation Ltd	Evening News (Edinburgh)	133 000
	Evening Express (Aberdeen)	77 000
D C Thompson	Evening Telegraph and Post (Dundee)	56 676

LIMITATIONS

Although Britain enjoys what could loosely be described as 'freedom of the press' there are certain limitations imposed on newspapers:

The law of libel Like anyone else in Britain, newspapers must ensure that they do not publish a statement which is defamatory, i.e. any article which brings a person into hatred, fear, ridicule or contempt. A lawyer is normally employed to check that the newspaper is not likely to be sued for libel.

Sub-judice rules During a trial, newspapers cannot comment in a way which might prejudice the fairness of the case. If the court considers that this has happened, then the newspaper could be held to be in contempt of court.

Official Secrets Acts (1899, 1911, 1920) These were introduced to prevent the publication of information from official sources which could endanger the country.

'D' Notices There is also a body called the Services, Press and Broadcasting Committee, which, on the advice of government, gives guidance to journalists on what can be published.

Other Acts of Parliament Newspapers must abide by laws in the same way as any other citizen. Examples of relevant laws are the Race Relations Act and the Sex Discrimination Act. There are also specific laws which affect advertising and some legal proceedings.

'Laws' of morality Many of these are not laws but conventions and are likely to change gradually.

The Press Council Unlike the other restraints mentioned, the Press Council has no legal authority. Newspapers accept that it will monitor their activities, as it has done since it was reconstituted in 1963. Its main aims are to deal with complaints by the public and to protect the freedom and reputation of the Press.

Public taste Newspapers are in business to make money and they can only do this if they sell as many copies as possible. Therefore, although at times they do try to shape public views, they are also attempting to reflect them. Editors must be guided by what they think their readers wish to see in their newspaper.

The Future of the Daily Graphic

Charlie Todd was not looking forward to the meeting with the owner, Lord Southfield. Sales of the *Daily Graphic* had dropped alarmingly in the last year, and he knew that, as editor, he was going to have to take some of the blame. He could not say it was all because of competition from television and the new commercial radio station. For some reason the circulation figures for his main rival, the *Morning Clarion*, were rising steadily. Mind you, they had a woman's supplement every day and a special colour magazine on Saturdays, so Charlie supposed these must be part of the attraction. But how did they manage to balance the books when his own showed that for each paper sold, there was a loss of one pence?

Cost per copy (pence)

Wages of reporters, printers, etc.	3.4
Paper, ink, etc.	6.0
Rates and rent	0.4
Power	0.2
Advertising	1.3
Distribution	1.8
Administration	0.8
	13.9

Income per copy (pence)

Sales of newspaper	8.0
Advertising in newspaper	4.9
	12.9

There were many things which the *Daily Graphic* had tried in the last couple of years. They had invested in new machinery – the very latest computer techniques (where did Lord Southfield get the money?) – and they had even persuaded the various chapels (or unions) to accept that at least some of the surplus workers would not be replaced. All this had been accompanied by the launching of a new style of *Daily Graphic* – they had gone over to tabloid – much more appealing to most people; they had kept the price of the paper below that of most of their competitors; they had even advertised on television. What they needed was a sensational scoop which could run for a few days so that new readers would stay with the paper.

One thing was for sure. Lord Southfield wasn't going to keep subsidising his beloved *Graphic* with the money from his successful hotels for ever. It looked like a shut-down . . . permanently. And who would employ the ex-editor of a bankrupt paper?

Questions

1 What are the main functions of the Press?   4
2 What can newspapers do that television cannot?   2
3 What are the main differences between a popular paper and a quality paper?   5
4 Comment on the different styles of reporting in the two articles on James Falconer's visit to the fête.   4
5 List the steps which a news item takes from the event to its appearance on the front page.   4
6 What are the duties of the Editor-in-Chief?   2
7 Make a table of the twenty-four newspapers mentioned, in order of popularity, under the following headings: newspaper; owner; circulation; style; area served.   10
8 What sort of articles and news items must a newspaper be careful not to print?   3
9 If a newspaper was losing money, what efforts could it make to improve its financial position?   4
10 What are the main differences between the front pages of each of the newspapers shown on page 29? Mention content, style, size.   10

Television and Radio

Television and radio are expected to fulfil the same functions as newspapers with the exception of 'influence'. Here they are expected, by Charter, to show 'balance and due impartiality in general presentation of programmes'.

Television

What is entertaining to one person may not be to another. For example, a ballet programme on BBC2 may be preferred by some people to a sports programme on BBC1 or ITV. BBC1 concentrates on family entertainment and programmes of wide appeal, while BBC2 puts greater emphasis on experiment and on serious cultural and documentary programmes, together with programmes for minority tastes.

BBC and IBA compete keenly for viewers and listeners, particularly at peak viewing times (early evening) when the largest audiences tune in.

Radio

BBC radio has four national stations, each attempting to provide a different service:

Radio 1   popular music
Radio 2   light music and sport
Radio 3   classical music and programmes of artistic and intellectual interest
Radio 4   UK news and information, with many speech programmes: drama, art, talks.

There are at the moment twenty local radio stations run by the BBC as well as nineteen independent or commercial stations. The BBC stations take part of the national programmes from Radio 4. The commercial stations such as Radio Clyde and Radio Forth provide a wide service of local news and information, various kinds of music and other entertainment, consumer advice and phone-ins.

ORGANISATION OF THE BRITISH BROADCASTING CORPORATION

The Chairperson and eleven Governors appointed by the Queen on the advice of the Government, have overall responsibility for programmes and equipment. They are advised by committees on special kinds of broadcasting, such as religious and schools, and by a Programme Complaints Commission. The governors appoint the Director General who is the chief executive officer.

The organisation of the BBC

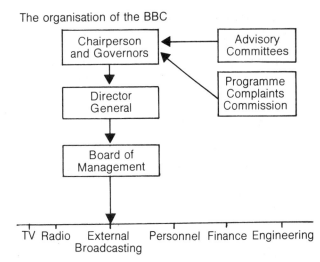

Each region produces its own local news service and other programmes, many of which are also shown or heard on the national network.

ORGANISATION OF THE INDEPENDENT BROADCASTING AUTHORITY

The IBA (Chairperson and ten members appointed by the Home Secretary) appoints commercial programme companies, supervises programmes, controls advertising and operates transmitting stations. It is advised by a General Advisory Council and specialist committees in the same way as the BBC, and has a Complaints Review Board. The Director General and his staff administer for the fifteen programme companies. A Network Planning Committee co-ordinates the supply, exchange and purchase of programmes.

Local commercial radio is controlled in the same way.

Each programme company produces its own

The organisation of the IBA

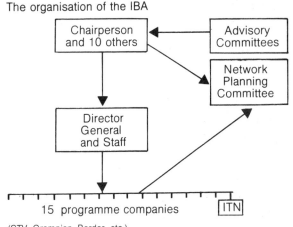

(STV, Grampian, Border, etc.)

news service, which may be sold to other companies or even the whole network. Commercial programme companies attempt to make a profit for their owners by having programmes which are popular enough to attract a large audience and therefore plenty of advertisers.

THE ANNAN COMMITTEE REPORT

In 1977 the Annan Committee produced a report on the future of broadcasting, which made two main proposals:
1 That responsibility for all local radio should be transferred from the BBC and the IBA to a new Local Broadcasting Authority.
2 That there should be a fourth television channel run by an Open Broadcasting Authority, which would include sponsored programmes, experimental programmes and minority interest programmes.

It is now at the Government's discretion to put forward proposals on these issues.

FINANCE

The BBC is financed by the sale of television licences – £10 for black and white and £25 for colour. In 1977 there were about eighteen million licenced television sets in Britain, and of these, ten million were colour sets. The BBC also receives grants from Parliament for external services, profits from BBC publications, including the *Radio Times*, and the export of television programmes.

Each of the IBA companies is financed by the sale of advertising time, the sale of programmes to other companies and the export of programmes. From this income they have to pay rental to the IBA for transmitting stations and a levy to the government which is related to profits.

Questions

1 What are the main differences between the programmes which appear on BBC1, BBC2 and ITV? 6
2 In what ways do commercial, local and national radio stations compete with each other? 6
3 What can the public do to complain about anything they see or hear on TV or radio? 3
4 Describe the programmes which might appear on an Open Broadcasting Authority station. 2
5 What efforts can the BBC make to keep down licence fees? 2
6 What efforts can IBA programme companies make to ensure a profit for their shareholders? 2
7 What are the three Scottish IBA programme companies? 1
8 Name as many of the other IBA TV companies as you can. What programmes, if any, does your ITV company take from them? 4

Letter to the *Glenforth Courier* – TV page

Dear Sir,
　　Last night on BBC1 there was a disgusting play with naked women and a lot of violence. Tonight's viewing has a film that was an 'X' in the cinema and repeat of an American detective series. ITV is just the same.
　　BBC2 has ballet and programmes about splitting the atom and current affairs.
　　I don't pay my TV licence for this sort of thing. I want entertainment. I think ordinary viewers should stop paying their licences. That would make the TV companies change their ways.

Yours, Jane Briggs (Mrs)

First of all, you'd only hit the BBC by not paying a licence, Mrs Briggs, and you'd be breaking the law, too. The IBA gets its money from adverts, so every time you buy beans or perfume you pay indirectly for IBA programmes.

The companies just don't have enough cash to produce new programmes every night – so you get repeats – but a lot of people ask to see programmes again. America buys some of our best programmes and we take theirs – gives a bit of variety. In our TV ratings item, you'll see some of the American series are very popular.

BBC2 is a special sort of channel for minority interests with documentaries, Open University programmes and items of interest to special groups of people like rugby fans or ballet or opera enthusiasts, but it also has pop music and hobby programmes.

The TV companies try very hard to keep family viewing hours free from 'adult' type plays and films (like the ones you are complaining about). They think most children will be in bed by the time they screen these -- at the end of the peak viewing time. If you feel very strongly about a programme you can write directly to the TV company's complaints department.

PART 2

The Economy

The Structure of a Mixed Economy

Firms and Money

The industries in a country can be owned and run by individuals who keep any profits made (and suffer any losses) and take whatever decisions they like on such questions as what, where, when and how to produce. This is sometimes known as 'free enterprise' economy.

Alternatively, industries can be owned and run by the Government on behalf of the people. Profits (and losses) are shared by the whole country and the answers to questions of production can take other issues into account. This is sometimes called 'State controlled' economy.

Britain's economy is somewhere in between – a 'mixed' economy. Some industries are owned privately (by shareholders) and some publicly (by Government). Governments of whatever political party try to influence both kinds of owners, indirectly through persuasion and grants and directly by laws. Governments also try to make sure that the British people receive the best possible standard of living. How this is to be done often leads to disagreements.

Start rent-free in a new factory

■ THE AREAS FOR EXPANSION

New Advance Factories are available in the Areas for Expansion.

Wide choice of locations and sizes

Rent-free period for up to 5 years in certain circumstances in Special Development Areas, and up to 2 years elsewhere, if enough new jobs are provided.

Rents assessed at current market value 99-year leases can be purchased.

Joe McPherson

Joe McPherson was a baker – a very good one, who sold his loaves to a number of local shops. He thought he might make more money if he could bake more bread by taking on extra workers and getting some new electric ovens. To do this he needed money and the bank wouldn't give him a big enough **loan**. His brother-in-law, Jimmy Cochrane, suggested that if they joined their money together and formed a partnership, Joe could expand his business. Joe asked his mother to put some money in as well, and though she agreed right away, Joe drew her a diagram of how the business worked (page 36).

The partnership worked – Joe had the extra money he needed and Jimmy was a skilled cake-maker. Part of the agreement was to change the name of the firm to 'McPherson and Cochrane'. Soon they were able to move to larger, modern premises at a low rent on an industrial estate.

With the success of the partnership, Joe thought of expanding further by forming a private limited company. He would offer **shares** in the company to the rest of his family: if the firm failed they would lose only the amount they had invested; if it succeeded they could earn interest on their shares in two ways. His mother, wanting to make sure of her income, bought stocks in the company. These gave her a fixed rate of interest, so that no matter what happened to the company's **profits** she would be guaranteed her income. Joe didn't think it showed much faith in the company! The rest of the family agreed to take ordinary shares which earned a dividend or income – usually the same every year, though in theory they could get more or less depending on the size of company profits.

With the extra **investment**, McPherson and Cochrane Ltd. went from strength to strength. Their range of products widened – they began printing labels, wrapping paper and boxes for their cakes and bread – 'diversification' Jimmy called it. He also thought it would be a good idea to move into grain farming and into transport too – so they would have control of earlier and later stages in the making and selling of bread. He gave this the grand title, 'vertical integration'.

Government advertisement to encourage firms to move to areas of high unemployment

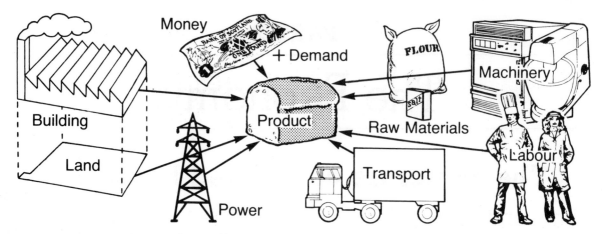

Necessary factors for production

Joe wasn't so happy about this. Where was the money for this extra investment to come from, since the family had no more? His bank manager suggested he make the company a public limited one and have shares sold on the Stock Exchange. This idea proved a success, as many investors, including some pension funds, saw the potential in McPherson and Cochrane Ltd.

The bakeries had become increasingly mechanised. Joe had problems every now and then with some of his employees. He sympathised with their complaint that standing beside a conveyor belt and doing the same task all day, every day was boring. Since each worker was skilled in his own job it was difficult to vary their tasks. Sometimes there were shortages of wrapping paper due to transport difficulties and if that happened, no bread was wrapped, the workers had to be laid off, and less bread was sold. Joe eventually worked out a deal with the unions which improved things. Both sides were happy with the concessions made — especially the new staff canteens.

In Britain, Joe discovered that the government and the EEC gave assistance to industries prepared to open factories in certain parts of the country with high unemployment (Assisted Areas). He got information about some of the loans and grants available.

After fifteen years they had become a **multi-national company**, with cakes and bread being made and sold throughout Europe, and almost every loaf of bread in Britain was made by McPherson and Cochrane. Competitors, apart from a few small businesses, had either been taken over or had given up. The Labour Government of the time began to wonder if such an important industry as bread-making should not be run and owned by the government on behalf of the nation. They said it would allow them to plan the economy better, if steel, coal and bread were government run. They also thought they could make a more efficient industry if it was nationalised, like electricity and gas, removing wasteful competition and ordering more research and development than Joe was prepared to do.

Joe was horrified at such interference. He wrote a very strong letter to the government saying that he was in favour of free enterprise, since nationalisation always meant more **bureaucracy** and paperwork; that nationalised industries were impersonal businesses which caused consumer dissatisfaction and laziness in workers; that people wouldn't be able to choose which bread to buy as there would be no competition and that the taxpayer would have to stump up, first to buy and then to subsidise the business. It was unfair that an Act of Parliament could remove his business from him and appoint a new board of directors responsible not to him and his shareholders, but to a minister of the government and Parliament. After all he had built it up from nothing.

Questions

1 In what three ways did Joe get extra money for his business? 3
2 If Joe had owned a men's clothes shop, what could he have done to a) diversify; b) vertically integrate? 4
3 Using the diagram, list the factors needed to produce something. Give an example of each factor. 4
4 What two things caused trouble between Joe and his workers? How could he have avoided these problems? 2
5 What help was the government prepared to offer Joe? Why? 2
6 What reasons might the government give for taking over the business? What would Joe's answers be? 4
7 What is the difference between free enterprise and nationalisation? 4
8 What changes would nationalisation bring to the running of Joe's business? 2

Industry

Industries in Britain can be grouped in various ways, depending on whether we are interested in who owns them; how they are organised; whether they are declining or expanding; or what they produce.

Who Owns Industry?

In private enterprise, a firm or industry, e.g. ICI or Fine Fare, is owned by individuals. Public enterprise or nationalisation means ownership of industry by the government on behalf of the nation, e.g. NCB or British Rail. In a mixed economy such as Britain there is a bit of both. The government also becomes involved in private enterprise by trying to improve industrial performance, by the use of taxes, grants, laws and advice.

How is it Organised?

An industry may be very small – one or two people who work for themselves, termed 'self-employed', e.g. joiners, small shopkeepers, or it may be very large, often using mass-production techniques, in which workers specialise in their own tasks. Mass-production, based on **economies of scale**, is efficient but can be boring for the employees.

Decline or Expansion?

Some industries have become less important to the economy than they were, in that they employ fewer people, or produce fewer goods, or are less likely to make a profit. They are known as declining industries, e.g. shipbuilding and steel. Expanding industries are those which are presumed to have a secure future, with an increasing **demand** for their product, e.g. oil and electronics.

What is Produced?

Industries can be divided into three types: primary industry produces raw materials which are either extracted from the ground or sea, e.g. mining, or grown in it, e.g. farming and forestry; secondary industry involves **manufacturing** raw material into something which can be sold to the consumer, e.g. clothing or steel; tertiary industry involves giving a service, e.g. hairdressing, transport, banking or **insurance**.

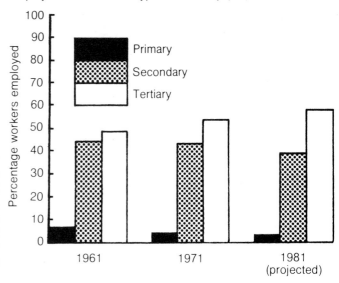

Employment in different types of industry (UK)

The Government and Industry

Governments, of whatever political party, try to involve themselves in the British economy. They are expected to assist in improving the efficiency and therefore the production performance of the economy as a whole and of different industries, in order to improve the standard of living of the country as a whole. Governments also try to solve such problems as unemployment and major differences in wealth between rich and poor people and rich and poor regions of Britian.

Nationalisation is one way in which a government can have greater control over an industry.

NATIONALISATION

If the government feels that an industry is so important to the well-being of the nation that the nation should control it, then it can nationalise the industry. This is Labour Party policy. The coal industry was nationalised in 1947 because the government felt it was the only way to modernise the industry. The railways were nationalised at the same time because they were seen to be an essential service where wasteful competition should be avoided and where, in many cases, services would have to be run at a loss. For example, if two separate railways ran between Edinburgh and Glasgow , it would be unlikely that both would make a profit. Nationalised industries

Table 7 Nationalised Industries

Industry		Year Nationalised
Coal	National Coal Board	1947
Electricity	Electricity Council	1947
Railways	British Railways Board	1947
Gas	Gas Corporation	1948
Steel	British Steel Corporation	1951 (denat. 1953–6 renat. 1967)
Transport	National Freight Corp.	1968
Post Office	Post Office Board	1969 (was gov. dept.)
Civil Aviation	British Airways	1971 (was BEA, BOAC)
Oil	British National Oil Corp.	1976
Shipbuilding	British Shipbuilders	1977
Aircraft	British Aerospace	1977

are run by a board appointed by the government minister concerned – the chairman and board of the NCB are appointed by the Minister of Energy. Every year the accounts and reports of the industries are examined by the House of Commons Select Committee on Nationalised Industries. Most of the nationalised industries try to 'break even'.

OTHER GOVERNMENT MEASURES

National Enterprise Board

Another way in which the government is involved in industry is through the National Enterprise Board (NEB) which was set up in 1975. It gives money to firms who are facing short-term problems, or it buys shares in firms, e.g. the NEB holds ninety-five per cent of British Leyland shares. This is called 'backdoor nationalisation' because the government has considerable control over what the company does with the money it is given and can also influence policy decisions. In Scotland, the Scottish Development Agency and the Highlands and Islands Development Board do similar work.

The Scottish Development Agency

The SDA was set up in 1975 with a budget of £300 million over five years. Its task was to spearhead the revival of Scottish industry. It has wide powers, including the building of factories, clearing land for industrial use and the power to make loans to, and invest in, private industry. By mid 1977, the SDA had spent £21 million on new factories, £19 million

on the reclamation of industrial land and £4 million on loans for investment in industry. Two major projects were the purchase of the St Enoch area of Glasgow, scheduled as the site for the new Ministry of Defence building with 7500 jobs, and the Glasgow Eastern Area Renewal Project – a huge **redevelopment** plan in what was described as the worst area of deprivation in Europe.

The Highlands and Islands Development Board

The Highlands and Islands Development Board was set up in 1965 to assist the Highlands and Islands. It gives loans and grants to industrial and commercial businesses, builds factories and can acquire land and set up businesses. An important part of its work is to encourage the development and improvement of **facilities** for tourists; for example, it helps with the setting up of craft industries and gives grants to help with the improvement of tourist accommodation.

Other ways in which governments try to improve industrial performance include:

Incentives such as grants and loans can be given to firms willing to move to certain areas in need of employment. These 'Assisted Areas' can benefit greatly from the influx of new and growing industries, sometimes replacing declining industries.

Taxation of corporations can be altered at different times, thus affecting the amount of money which a firm can dispose of in its own way.

Taxation of individuals, either directly, through income tax, or indirectly through taxes such as VAT, can be changed to allow the buying public more or less money to spend at any time.

Money for borrowing by firms (credit) can be made more or less easy to obtain.

Laws can be passed to control conditions of work (hours of work, safety, early retirement), mergers and the creation of monopolies.

Governments can alter the amount of money which they spend on behalf of the public. For example, more money allocated to education can mean more business for book publishers.

Together the state industries shown on page 39 had a deficit of £700 million in 1975, a deficit of £200 million in 1976 and a surplus of about £500 million in 1977. All the industries had been affected by the **recession**. Companies were buying less steel from the British Steel Corporation, therefore

State industries climbing back to profit

£m	1974	1975	1976	1977
PROFIT				
300				POST OFFICE†
200				ELECTRICITY*†
			POST OFFICE	
100	BRITISH STEEL · BRITISH AIRWAYS · NATIONAL BUS · NAT. FREIGHT	BRITISH STEEL	BRITISH GAS · ELECTRICITY*	BRITISH AIRWAYS† · BRITISH GAS† · NAT. COAL BOARD · NATIONAL BUS
(profit line)		NAT. COAL BOARD	NAT. COAL BOARD	
LOSS				
	BRITISH GAS · BRITISH RAIL	BRITISH AIRWAYS · NAT. FREIGHT · NATIONAL BUS · BRITISH GAS	BRITISH AIRWAYS · NATIONAL BUS · NAT. FREIGHT · BRITISH RAIL	NAT. FREIGHT · BRITISH RAIL
100	POST OFFICE · NAT. COAL BOARD · ELECTRICITY*	BRITISH RAIL		BRITISH STEEL
200		ELECTRICITY*	BRITISH STEEL	
300		POST OFFICE		

*Electricity Council, England & Wales only   †Forecast

less coal was needed for the steel works from the National Coal Board. This in turn meant less business for British Rail which transported the coal from the NCB mines to the BSC works. They were also badly hit by the government's price controls in 1974–75, when they could only increase prices if they could show an unavoidable rise in costs.

The 1977 surplus was partly due to the government's wage restraint policy which helped keep the wages bill down and partly due to some industries, such as British Airways, benefiting from the fall in the value of the pound (which attracted foreign travellers). Since many of the state industries are monopolies, it is hard to say whether or not they are becoming more efficient because there is nothing to compare them with, but some, such as the National Freight Corporation, are growing more competitive.

Questions

1 Using the table of employment in different types of industry, which type of industry is growing fastest? Which type of industry is the least important?   2
2 Why could the government be blamed for the nationalised industries making a loss in 1974–5 but a profit in 1977?   2
3 If a nationalised industry makes a profit, why could this be a bad sign?   2
4 Why does government get involved in the British economy?   3
5 If an industry is nationalised, what control does the government have over its operation?   3
6 The work of the National Enterprise Board is often called 'backdoor nationalisation'. Why?   2
7 What does the Scottish Development Agency try to do?   3
8 What two areas of the highland economy does the Highlands and Islands Development Board pay particular attention to?   2

Selected Industries

Machine operators in a computer factory

Table 8 Employment in selected industries (mid 1976) (*Dept. of Employment Gazette*)

Industry	Great Britain	Scotland
Agriculture	360 000	41 600
Coal mining	297 500	27 800
Food and drink manufacture	660 000	90 800
Chemicals	420 700	28 600
Metal manufacture	468 100	39 100
Shipbuilding	175 400	42 300
Cars, etc.	446 200	18 300
Construction	1 269 000	171 000
Railways	218 100	20 500
Wholesale distribution	526 000	38 700
Retailing	1 850 600	178 300
Education	1 834 000	165 000
Health Service	1 250 400	142 800
National government administration	662 700	52 600
Miscellaneous services	2 252 000	226 700

ELECTRONICS

Electronics is Scotland's fastest growing industry. IBM, Ferranti, Burroughs, Honeywell and Hughes Microelectronics are among the major firms which moved to Scotland after 1965 because of the incentives the government offered. A wide variety of products are made in Scotland, including security and radar systems, ultra-sonic equipment for medical diagnosis, accounting machines and consumer goods such as stereo equipment and television sets.

Forty thousand workers are employed in factories spread throughout the Central Lowlands, many of which are subsidiaries of American-owned companies.

COAL

Coal is one of the foundations on which Scotland's industrial revolution was based, and is still an important source of power and raw material.

The Labour Government of 1945–51 considered that coal was so important to Britain that it was nationalised in 1947, and put under the management of the National Coal Board (present Chairman Derek Ezra), which is responsible to the Minister for Energy and to Parliament.

From the 1950s to the early 1970s there was a fall in demand for coal, due mainly to changing tastes, the creation of smokeless zones, the abandonment of steam power on the railways, the discovery of natural gas to replace coal gas, and competition from other fuels, especially oil. Since the 1950s many uneconomic pits have been closed and advanced mining machines, self-advancing powered roof supports and improved underground transport have led to a further reduction in employment.

Since the energy crisis of 1973, coal has again become an important fuel. Enormous reserves –

Coal consumption in the UK (NCB only)

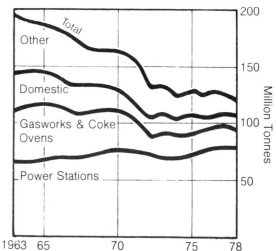

Remote control of underground plant and mining operations

over 8000 million tonnes – are estimated to be economically viable, and after a long period of decline in employment in mining, there is now a risk of a shortage of skilled miners.

In Scotland, twenty-three pits, mainly in Fife, Ayrshire and the Lothians, employ 27 800 men. The South of Scotland Electricity Board is the NCB's main customer and takes seventy per cent of the coal mined. Some is used to feed the big coal-fired power stations at Kincardine, Cockenzie (which is fed by a merry-go-round train from Monktonhall) and Longannet. The Longannet complex is the most sophisticated: it has a nine-kilometre conveyor belt which collects coal from three linked mines and brings it to the surface near the power station. A central computer helps to

Table 9 NCB employment and output (*Britain 1979, HMSO*)

	Employees	Output (million tonnes)
1913	1 000 000+	287
1955	700 000	220
1960	549 000	194
1965	419 000	188
1970	286 000	143
1975	248 000	125
1977	242 000	119
1978	240 000	119
1985	——	167 (projected)

control the flow of coal and regulates the correct mix of qualities so that the power station is fed with a consistent blend.

CHEMICALS

The chemical industry is one of the fastest growing British industries, especially since the discovery and exploitation of North Sea oil. It accounts for over eleven per cent of British exports. Products include fertilisers, dyes, paints, drugs, explosives, building materials, fibres, plastics, and chemicals, which are the raw materials for other industries like detergents, glass and metals.

The refinery at Grangemouth is the largest supplier of petrochemical products in Britain – these form the basis of synthetic fibres, detergents, drugs and synthetic rubber. Many manufacturers have set up close to the refinery and pipe their raw materials directly from it. The development of North Sea oil has stimulated the petrochemical side of the industry at a time when the world recession meant a fall in demand for other products.

The biggest new project in Scotland – an Esso ethylene cracker plant at Mossmorran in Fife – was given the go-ahead in 1978 after a long public inquiry.

STEEL

Steel is a basic material from which many other products are made in the areas of transport, building, machinery, tools, consumer goods and engineering.

In 1967, the British Steel Corporation was created to manage the fourteen companies which had been nationalised for a second time. Eighty-five per cent of Britain's crude steel is produced by the BSC which employs 220 000 people (21 000 in Scotland). The private-sector companies produce about one-third of the value (fifteen per cent by volume) of the industry's turnover, employ 68 000 people, and are mainly involved in finished products.

In the last few years the steel industry has been badly hit by a world-wide recession. Its overseas **markets**, as well as the domestic ones, have shrunk and have been faced not only with long-standing competition from the USA, Japan and Europe but also from new steel makers in Brazil, India and Korea, which have modern plants, and fewer, lower-paid workers.

The 1973 Plan for Steel was a ten-year one to modernise and expand production capacity. Older

An electric-arc furnace in operation at Sheerness Steel Works

open-hearth steelmaking was to be replaced by the basic oxygen process for bulk production and the electric arc process for specialised steel. However, by late 1977, BSC was losing £1 million per day and each ton of steel made was being sold at a loss of £23.

The British Steel Corporation is faced with very difficult decisions on Scottish steelmaking. A large part of west central Scotland – centres like Motherwell, Bellshill, Glengarnock and Craigneuk – relies on steelmaking and if the steelworks close it tears the heart out of the place. For example, a recent Government White Paper proposed that steelmaking should end at Glengarnock and that the works should produce only narrow plate, for use in ships and bridge-building. This would reduce the workforce from 1000 to 250 and make Glengarnock's unemployment rate rise to thirty per cent. The 'social cost' – hardship to families – would be high even if money could be saved by not

using an out-of-date steelworks. The Paper also suggested shelving proposals for a huge integrated steelworks at Hunterston on the Clyde, on the grounds that there would not be enough work for it. There is to be an ore-terminal and perhaps a steelmaking plant on the site.

However, some old-fashioned plants have to be closed because they are too expensive to operate, and there is a limit to the money available for modernisation or completely new works. Some people have to lose their jobs since less steel is being made. Redundancy payments make unemployment a bit more acceptable to people and their unions. Other countries are facing the same problem of shrinking sales, and are trying desperately to sell their steel to our old customers.

Modern, efficient integrated works like Ravenscraig, with electric-arc steelmaking, are the key to the future so BSC is prepared for a possible future rise in demand for steel.

BRITISH RAIL

In 1973, the government and the British Railways Board completed a review of railway policy and agreed that the only way to keep the railway network going and maintain the quality of service was for the government to give substantial financial support.

The most important development in recent years has been the replacement of steam trains by diesel and then electric trains. The standard of track and signalling have been improved to meet the new faster running speeds.

One improvement in passenger transport has been the 'Inter-City' services emphasising speed, reliability, comfort and better connections. Commuter services, however, tend to lose money. The new Advanced Passenger Train capable of speeds of 250k/h (155mph) entered service between London and Glasgow in 1978 with a journey time of four hours.

The most important freight traffic is in coal, coke, iron and steel. A computer now monitors all consignments and freight movements and allows for more intensive use of rolling stock. BR want to attract more whole-trainload freight traffic, such as cars going nightly from Linwood to the Midlands of England. Container services are operated by Freightliners Ltd – a company owned jointly by the National Freight Corporation and British Rail. The introduction of such mechanisation has increased the ability of BR to assist firms, and the whole economy of Britain.

BR are, however, faced with four long-term problems:

Passengers BR often operates as a service, whose main aim may not be to make a profit. Many commuters would not use trains if the full fare was charged. Remote areas, such as the north of Scotland, would be even more isolated if lines were closed just because they lost money. This did happen to some extent after 1963, when the Beeching Plan saw the reshaping and **rationalising** of rail transport.

Freight When the economy is in recession and less is being produced, less is transported. Moreover, much of the equipment and methods are out of date.

Costs Wages make up sixty-six per cent of the total costs. The railway is a very labour intensive industry, especially in track maintenance and signalling, and overmanning is a problem both in office-staffing and in the use of guards and firemen.

Competition Lorries have the advantage over rail-freight in providing door-to-door service. Airlines are, on the whole, quicker. Cars are more personal and are subsidised in that they do not pay the full cost of roads. Off-peak and special fares attract some extra passengers, but not enough.

MOTOR VEHICLES

The British motor vehicle industry represents ten per cent of Britain's total exports; it prevents the importing of more foreign cars; it employs 500 000 workers directly, with a further 500 000 dependent on it. Traditionally the industry is based in the Midlands of England and ninety-eight per cent of British cars are produced by four companies: British Leyland (157 000 workers); Ford (an American-owned company with 70 000 workers); Vauxhall (American, 28 000); and the Talbot Car Co. (French, 23 000).

The motor industry in Scotland dates from the early 1960s, when two motor plants were built in Scotland as a result of government policy to encourage factories to areas of high unemployment. Rootes (later Chrysler UK) opened a factory at Linwood, employing 8000, and BLMC opened a truck-making factory at Bathgate, in addition to their Scotstoun works, employing a total of 10 000.

The industry depends on as many as four hundred component parts, made in smaller factories. The parts are assembled by a skilled engineering labour force on a conveyer belt system, designed to achieve economies of scale.

A trainload of cars
from Talbot, Linwood

Sunbeam assembly line, Talbot, Linwood

Three of the four major companies are owned by multi-national concerns who may have different interests from those which benefit Britain, e.g. Ford, General Motors (Vauxhall), Talbot.
Productivity has been low relative to foreign companies.
Models have often proved less popular than those of foreign competitors.
Luxury cars, such as Rover and Jaguar, have been in demand but production bottlenecks have meant long waiting lists.
Industrial relations **disputes**, often unofficial, have proved disruptive.
The reputation for quality, delivery dates and after-sales service has declined.
Inflation has affected costs, e.g. a standard Mini in 1959 cost £486, in 1966 £515, in 1975 £1299 and in 1978 £2016.

British Leyland, created by merger in 1968, and taken over by the National Enterprise Board in 1975, has found things particularly difficult as it is the only completely British firm, and is unable to rely on foreign parts. It has recently been reorganised so that decisions can be taken more quickly in each of its four trading areas – cars, trucks and buses, special parts, and international.

Chrysler UK 'collapsed' in 1965 and was rescued by the government, who put £162 million into the firm. Part of the blame for the firm's troubles went to poor performance at Linwood (including bad industrial relations). Avenger production was moved to Linwood from Coventry and a new model, the Sunbeam, was launched from the Linwood lines. The future of Chrysler UK and Linwood seemed more certain only for a short time as in mid 1978, news came of a take over of Chrysler's European interests by the French firm, Peugeot–Citröen: after that the company was called Talbot.

SHIPBUILDING

Britain has a long shipbuilding tradition and has the fifth largest shipbuilding industry in the world. The industry was nationalised in 1977 and the new British Shipbuilders includes the larger shipbuilding and repairing companies, and some marine engine manufacturers. The remaining private sector makes smaller vessels, like pleasure craft and patrol boats as well as drilling ships and oil rigs.

With world shipbuilders, the British industry is facing the worst recession for almost forty years. The world shipping market has collapsed – buyers no longer want new luxury liners (travel in this way is less fashionable now) or oil tankers (when oil

However, production can be disrupted if parts are not delivered on time for any reason. The assembly line work is thought to be repetitive and tedious. Demarcation (who does what) disputes are common and workers feel insecure because the demand for cars fluctuates and therefore demand for labour changes.

For many years the demand for cars was high, but now the world recession has left a twenty-five per cent overcapacity in car manufacturing in Europe. Competition from abroad has increased, especially from Japan which, in 1978, took eleven per cent of the British market. For a car to be successful, it must be cheap to produce and to run, reliable in delivery and performance, and profitable for the maker.

Some of the major problems for the British industry have been:

A Polish ship under construction at Govan Shipbuilders Ltd

prices rose sharply in 1973, the sales of oil fell so that fewer tankers were needed). Foreign competition is fierce, especially from super-efficient Japan, with fifty per cent of the market, and India, Korea and Sweden. Inflation has also hit the order books – orders placed at a fixed price, allowing for ten per cent inflation, meant building at a loss when the inflation rate reached twenty-five to thirty per cent.

All this has meant that Britain has had to reorganise her shipbuilding industry. In 1966 the Geddes Report recommended restructuring of the industry into large groupings. Some of these were successful; others, like Upper Clyde Shipbuilders faced many problems – lack of orders, industrial disputes, overmanning, old-fashioned production methods, restrictive practices (rules about which and how many workers worked) and rising costs of raw materials. Nationalisation should give the government more control over rationalisation (the closing of old-fashioned yards and ending of wasteful processes). More control over the subsidisation of orders (e.g. the 1978 deal with Poland) might also help.

In Scotland the industry now employs 42 300. The most important groups are Scott Lithgow at

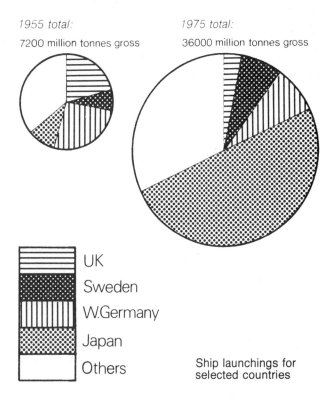

1955 total:
7200 million tonnes gross

1975 total:
36000 million tonnes gross

UK
Sweden
W.Germany
Japan
Others

Ship launchings for selected countries

Greenock and Port Glasgow (Lower Clyde Shipbuilders), Govan Shipbuilders and Yarrow which emerged from Upper Clyde Shipbuilders, and Robb Caledon on the east coast.

The Clyde shipyards are as competitive as any in Europe. Govan shipbuilders specialise in series production – planning one ship in great detail, then building others which are identical. Scott Lithgow can build a wide range of vessels but have new facilities for building giant ships and 'stitching' them together at the quayside. Though this idea was first meant for giant tankers, it can be used to build other types of vessel, e.g. offshore oil storage facilities. A sign of the times is that the former John Brown's at Clydebank, where the elegant *Queens* were built, now builds for the oil industry.

AGRICULTURE

The type of farming carried out in any part of Britain depends first upon the type of soil and the weather. The wetter west grows rich grass, good for cattle rearing, but has too little sun to ripen grains like wheat and barley (although researchers are trying to develop varieties which will ripen with less sun). The drier and sunnier east is more suitable for arable or crop farming. Hilly areas are suitable only for sheep. Most farms in Britain are mixed farms, with both livestock rearing and arable farming. This enables the farmer to make best use of his land and avoid 'putting all his eggs in one basket'.

Secondly, the type of farming depends on markets. Vegetable growing is widespread near big cities where it is the market, not the soil or climate, that is most important. The rearing of battery chickens or stall-fed animals is also linked to a market rather than to soil or climate. Fruit farming depends on markets but also needs sunny weather so is more restricted. Because of the mild winters and early springs, the southwest of England is able to specialise in early fruit, vegetables and flowers.

Scottish farming

The most important products of Scottish farms are livestock products – mutton, lamb and wool being the 'growth' industry. Hills, as well as being the main area for sheep, are also the rearing ground for the basic stock of the lowland farmers – cattle and sheep which are fattened on the richer lowland pastures. Barley, field vegetables and soft fruit are increasingly important (Scotland is Europe's

Industry in the Central Lowlands of Scotland

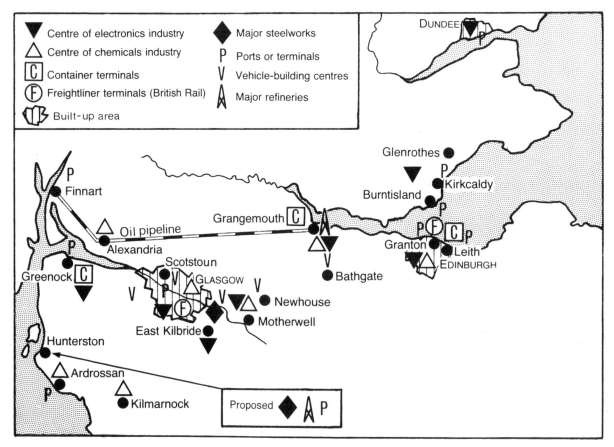

Scotland: main types of agriculture

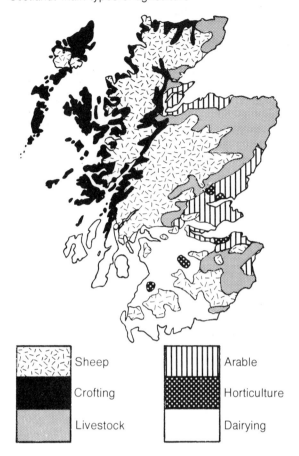

Sheep

Crofting

Livestock

Arable

Horticulture

Dairying

leading raspberry grower). Barley has replaced oats as the major crop and now occupies more than two-thirds of the cropping area – it is used for the malting and brewing industries at home and in Europe. Potatoes, both for human consumption and as seed for English potato growers are very important, too. Horticulture – fruit, flower and vegetable growing – has increased both in the area of land it uses and in the value of its products.

Farming methods

Farms today are more mechanised and employ fewer workers than farms twenty years ago. Fields have been made larger to enable very large machines like combine harvesters to operate. The plants themselves have been altered by selective breeding so that they grow to the same height and ripen at the same time so that machine harvesting is possible. New varieties can withstand wetter or harsher climates and pesticides, insecticides and fertilisers ensure that the crops are as near perfect as possible when harvested.

Livestock rearing is mechanised too. Cows, specially bred to have high milk yields, are milked by machine on revolving milking platforms while being fed specially mixed feed. Hens are reared indoors in batteries where heating, lighting and feeding are controlled to give high egg production. Veal calves live their short lives in slatted floored pens and are fed milk to keep their flesh white. These and other artificial methods of rearing animals are called factory farming and are criticised by many people who feel it is unnatural, cruel and produces tasteless food.

This all means that it costs a great deal of money to operate a farm. Bills for electricity, livestock feed, fertilisers and other chemicals are high. Wage rates for farm workers, which in the past were always low, are coming closer to those of industrial workers. The cost of modern farming equipment and up-to-date buildings for housing animals and storing crops is very high and has been made worse by inflation.

The Government and the farmer

The government helps the farmer in many ways. Apart from research centres and agricultural colleges, which provide technical and scientific assistance and investigate new strains of plants and breeds of animals, it also provides a wide range of grants and loans to help the farmer with major expenses, such as draining land, building new storage facilities and buying new equipment. It also negotiates for the farmers at the EEC Council of Ministers.

The farmer and the EEC

As a member of the European Economic Community, Britain is subject to its Common Agricultural Policy. This aims to abolish barriers to trade in agricultural products between member countries; to stabilise markets to stop sudden shortages or gluts of produce and to give shoppers quality food at reasonable prices.

Every year all the EEC countries agree on a price for each agricultural product, which will give farmers a reasonable income. This is the Target Price. If the price of a product falls eight per cent below this (if, for example, more of the product has been produced than expected), then the EEC buys up the suplus at this Intervention Price, and stores the product. Imported food is taxed with an Import Levy so that it is more expensive than a similar EEC product.

The food that is bought up by the EEC has been

nicknamed 'mountains' and 'lakes'. There have been butter mountains, milk-powder mountains, sugar mountains and wine lakes. These mountains and lakes are a sign that the Common Agricultural Policy is not working perfectly yet.

Since each EEC country has its own currency – British pound, Italian lira, etc. – a special currency was invented to make payments between EEC countries easier. This is called the 'Green Rate'. The exchange rate in green currencies is agreed by the Council of Ministers. So we pay our EEC agricultural bills in green pounds, the French pay theirs in green francs.

Questions

1 Using the industries named in Table 8, group them according to each of the four ways of classifying industries. 4
2 Which three industries are the largest employers in Britain? Compare this with the three largest employers for Scotland. 3

3 What sort of work is done in a typical electronics factory? (Mention: worker, scale of work, skill required, product.) 4

4 Explain why the demand for coal a) fell from 1950s to early 1970s (see graph on p. 40); b) rose after 1973. 3
5 Describe the operation of a modern coal mine. (Mention: workforce, conditions of work, machinery, skill required, output, product. Table 9 will help.) 4
6 What would be the likely arguments stated at the public inquiry:
   a) for the new plant at Mossmorran;
   b) against the new plant at Mossmorran? (Mention: jobs, raw materials, markets, pollution, Grangemouth). 5

7 For what reasons has the British Steel Corporation been losing money in recent years? 4
8 What problems face the BSC when it wants to close an out-of-date steelworks? 3
9 Why is it important to keep modern efficient steelworks operating? 1

10 Why does the government give money to British Rail? 2
11 In what ways has British Rail tried to improve passenger services? 3
12 In what ways has British Rail tried to improve freight services? 3

13 What are the major problems facing British Rail today? How might they be solved? 6

14 Give three reasons why the motor vehicle industry is important to Britain. 3
15 What problems are facing the motor vehicle industry in Britain? 6
16 Describe the problems facing a worker in the motor vehicle factory at Linwood. 3
17 In what ways has the government helped the motor vehicle industry? 3

18 Using the pie charts of ship launchings (page 45), compare the performance of British shipyards for 1955 and 1975 with that of other countries. 6
19 Why is Britain finding it difficult to sell ships? 3
20 What attempts were made to improve the shipbuilding industry's performance? 4
21 Describe the work of a modern Scottish shipyard. (Mention: materials used, skills needed and products.) 4

22 What is the main type of farming carried out in your area? 1
23 Why is this type of farming important in your area? 2
24 In what ways has Scottish farming changed in recent years? Mention types of farming and methods. 6
25 What are the arguments for and against factory farming? 4
26 How does the government help the farmer? Why? 3
27 What are the aims of the Common Agricultural Policy? 3
28 In what ways does CAP try to ensure a) that a farmer receives a reasonable income; b) that he is protected from cheap foreign produce? 4
29 What is the 'green pound'? 2

30 Using the map of central Scotland, explain why a light-engineering firm, producing domestic consumer goods, would choose to set up its factory there. 3

Scotland: main communication links and towns mentioned in the text ▶

48

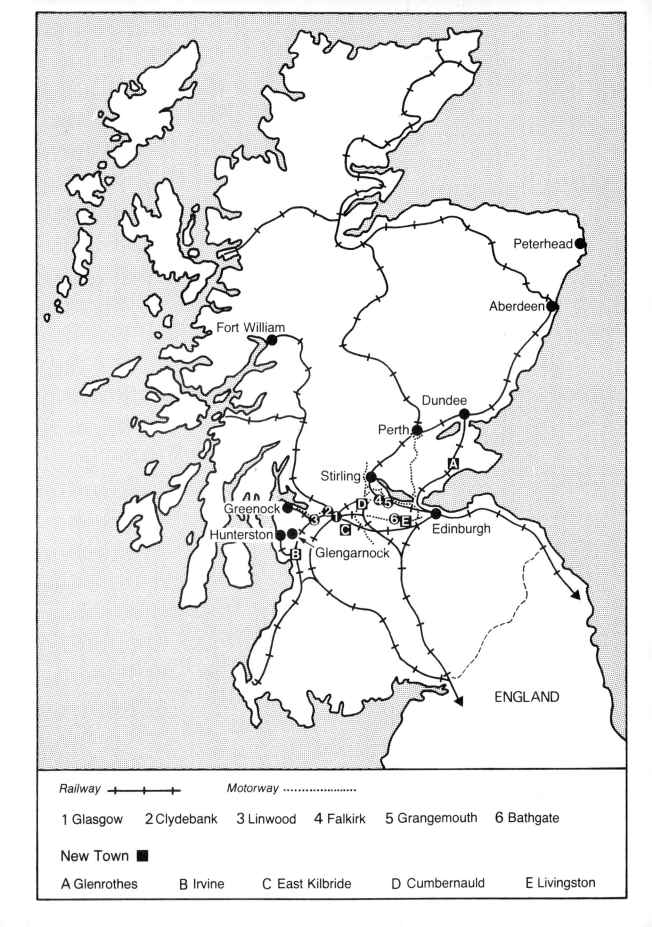

Peterhead

Aberdeen

Fort William

Dundee

Perth

Stirling

Greenock

Hunterston

D 4 5

C

6 **E**

Edinburgh

3 2 1

B Glengarnock

ENGLAND

Railway ┼─┼─┼   *Motorway* ....

1 Glasgow   2 Clydebank   3 Linwood   4 Falkirk   5 Grangemouth   6 Bathgate

New Town ■

A Glenrothes   B Irvine   C East Kilbride   D Cumbernauld   E Livingston

A modern Job Centre

Unemployment

To most people, the word 'unemployed' means being out of work, looking for work, capable of work and available for work. Each month the Department of Employment issues figures to show the level of unemployment in Britain. The higher the figures are, the more concerned the public and the government become. Both are anxious that unemployment should be kept as low as possible, and certainly below the level of the 1930s when more than one in five of the population was out of work at times.

It is accepted that zero per cent unemployment is impossible to achieve because there are always some people who are changing jobs and are therefore temporarily unemployed, and some who are, for one reason or another reluctant to find work. This latter category might include housewives who are happy to stay at home; the mothers of young children; the rich and the lazy. Some people are unemployable, e.g. schoolchildren, the old, and the severely mentally or physically handicapped. Most of these groups are not usually included in the figures of unemployment.

THE EFFECTS OF UNEMPLOYMENT

Unemployment means that one of the country's most important **resources** (labour) is not being fully used. This is as inefficient as not using all available farm land, or not mining all available coal in a mine.

Unemployment means that some people are not helping to create things which can be sold and which can therefore put more money into the economy. People in work have a higher standard of living and can therefore buy more goods and services, which in turn means more jobs for more people.

The loss of dignity involved in being unemployed, especially if it is long-term, is harmful to individuals and their families.

Unemployment benefits and other sums of money paid to the unemployed and their families have to be met from government revenue.

TYPES OF UNEMPLOYMENT: WHAT CAN HELP?

Frictional (People temporarily out of work.)

a) Make it easier for people to see what alternative jobs are available by providing easier access to more information about vacancies.

b) Job Centres give information about vacancies. They are more attractive than the old Employment Exchanges, are easier to find, and are without the stigma of the dole queue of the 1930s.

Seasonal (People who perform short-term jobs for a 'season' or part of the year.)

a) Encourage firms which employ seasonal workers to diversify so that they can provide regular employment. Tourist centres could, for example, try to become all year round attractions.
b) Attempts could be made to make work less dependant on the weather. The building industry sometimes uses prefabrication methods, where sections of houses are built in a factory and assembled on site. Some shipyards have begun to arrange for parts of ships, or even whole ships, to be built indoors.

Technological (People whose jobs are taken over by new machinery or automation.)

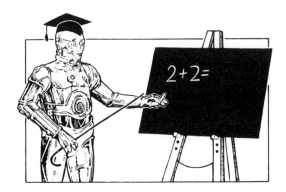

a) Workers made redundant by new techniques could be retrained to give them a new skill.

b) Workers could refuse to work with new machines if it meant creating more unemployment. This could lead, however, to hidden unemployment, in the form of job sharing, overmanning and restrictive practices.

Structural (People whose jobs have been made irrelevant by a change in the structure of the economy.)

a) Resist the change in the structure of the economy by arranging for someone like the government to prop up the part which no one else wants.
b) Anticipate the change by shifting resources, such as newly trained workers, to meet the new conditions.

Cyclical (People whose job is caught in a slump when no one can afford to buy their goods or services.)

a) Make sure more money is available for people to spend, thus raising the demand for goods and services. This could be done by such measures as lowering direct taxation to make goods relatively cheaper or by making it easier for people to borrow money to spend.
b) Try to even out the booms and slumps in the economy by ensuring that the good times are not too good and the bad times are not too bad.

Number of people unemployed 1960–79

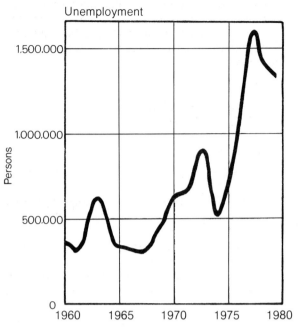

Unemployment

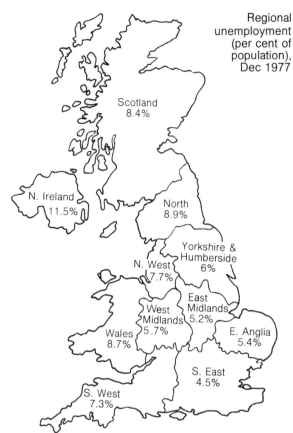

Regional unemployment (per cent of population), Dec 1977

Scotland 8.4%

N. Ireland 11.5%

North 8.9%

Yorkshire & Humberside 6%

N. West 7.7%

East Midlands 5.2%

West Midlands 5.7%

Wales 8.7%

E. Anglia 5.4%

S. East 4.5%

S. West 7.3%

It will be seen that in most of these possible solutions the government would have to act. Increasingly it has been seen as the government's role to intervene in the running of the economy to ensure as near full employment as possible. However, if full employment is achieved, other problems may arise which can only be solved by the deliberate creation of some unemployment. To take just one example, if too many people have too much money because they are all fully employed, this could lead to inflation.

Table 10 Regional unemployment – Scotland, March 1979 (*Manpower Services Commission*)

Region	Total number	Percentage
Highland	8 026	10.8
Grampian	9 043	5.0
Tayside	13 517	7.9
Fife	10 189	7.5
Strathclyde	103 694	9.5
Lothians	22 245	6.6
Central	7 851	6.9
Dumfries and Galloway	4 683	8.7
Borders	1 735	4.5
Shetland	244	3.4
Orkney	400	6.3
Western Isles	1 370	16.7
Scotland	182 997	8.3
Great Britain	1 402 254	5.7

Questions

1 Why will there always be some unemployment? 2
2 Why is unemployment 'a bad thing'? 4
3 What can make a person unemployed? 5
4 What can the government do to try to reduce unemployment? Is it likely to be successful? 10
5 What has happened to the numbers of people unemployed in Britain since 1960? 4
6 Which regions of Britain have the highest unemployment? Why might this be the case? 5
7 On a map of Scotland, mark the unemployment by region using the following shadings: unemployment rate over 10% – solid shading; unemployment rate between 5.1% and 9.9% – striped shading; unemployment rate 5% and below – dots. 10
8 Explain the low unemployment rate in the regions you have shaded with dots. 3
9 What efforts can an individual make to prevent him/herself being unemployed? 3

Inflation

Inflation is the increase in price of goods and services as a result of a fall in the buying-power of money. To most people it means they cannot buy as much as they used to.

The Retail Price Index is used as a measure of inflation. The cost of purchasing a 'basket' or collection of goods, including food, clothing, plus housing and transport costs, is calculated each month. Over months and years, this shows the change in the buying-power of the pound.

THE EFFECT OF INFLATION

People are able to buy less when prices are rising fast, so fewer people are needed to produce things. This leads to unemployment.

People who live on fixed incomes which cannot be easily raised, such as pensioners, find it increasingly difficult to make ends meet. This can lead to great hardship for many.

If British-made goods become more expensive to sell, then exporting British goods becomes more difficult, unless other countries have a high rate of inflation as well. Moreover, people in Britain may start to buy foreign-made goods if they are cheaper.

There is a fear that if prices rise extremely fast and Britain enters a period of hyperinflation, then people will lose all confidence in the use of money. This can happen if people are afraid that money will be worth less in the future than in the present. They then try to get rid of the money by buying things and will be prepared to spend more than usual in order to have something which will keep its value. When this begins to happen on a grand scale, money may cease to be used altogether and people will only be able to get goods in exchange for other goods (bartering).

Cost increases are passed on to the consumer in the form of higher prices

If a government can identify the main causes of inflation then it can begin to encourage or enforce measures which will cure or solve inflation. However, it must be noted that possible solutions to inflation may create problems in other areas of the economy.

TYPES OF INFLATION: WHAT CAN HELP?

'Cost push'

Use cheaper raw materials, e.g. chicory instead of coffee beans.

Find domestic alternatives to imported raw materials, e.g. North Sea oil instead of Arab oil or South American oil.

Control wage increases, either by a wage freeze or by an incomes policy.

Reduce income tax so that people have more money to spend and do not need a wage increase.

Reduce VAT so that goods and services become instantly cheaper.

Check price increases against costs and profits, e.g. by the Price Commission.

Limit profits so that they must be channelled back into companies in the form of cost-reducing investment.

Encourage people to buy in bulk and shop around.

Encourage companies to increase efficiency by 'Save It' campaigns, incentives and manpower reductions.

'Demand pull'

Encourage people to save rather than spend, e.g. by raising interest rates.

Make it harder for people to borrow money to spend, e.g. by raising interest rates on bank loans, creating a credit squeeze.

Consumers who have more money may be prepared to demand goods at a higher price

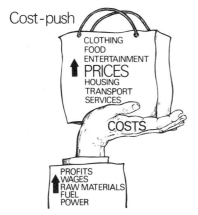

Cost-push

CLOTHING
FOOD
ENTERTAINMENT
↑ PRICES
HOUSING
TRANSPORT
SERVICES

COSTS

↑ PROFITS
WAGES
RAW MATERIALS
FUEL
POWER

Demand-pull ↑ SPENDING PAST SAVINGS
↑ SPENDING HIGHER INCOMES

DEMAND

BUS FARES
RECORDS
HOTEL BILLS
↑ PRICES
WASHING MACHINES
CLOTHES
CINEMA TICKETS
FOOTWEAR
RENT

Restrict hire purchase agreements by increasing the minimum deposit, shortening repayment periods, and/or raising the interest rate so that people are more reluctant to take up such agreements.

Increase taxation so that people have less to spend.

Cut government-spending on roads, education, defence, health, etc.

Keep down increases in income by a wage freeze or incomes policy.

Table 11 A typical shopping basket

	Price (pence)	
Item	1975	1978 (Feb.)
1 doz. eggs	35	50
1 pint milk	4½	12
White loaf	13½	21½
1 lb butter	28	54
8 oz jar coffee	73½	£2.15
¼ lb tea	10	25½
6 chocolate biscuits	18	27
1 lb cheddar cheese	42	78
E3 size washing powder	28	55½
16 oz tin tomato soup	11½	15
1 lb pork sausages	33½	47½
1 lb mince	42	58
1 lb brussels sprouts	10	14
1 lb whiting	49	94
½ lb margarine	9	12½
1 bottle orange squash	23	27½
1 tin peaches	19	25
large tube toothpaste	12	30

Money supply

Stop the government from borrowing money to spend.

Prevent the Bank of England from printing more

The rate of inflation 1963–79

More money becomes available to people so they are prepared to spend more to buy the same goods

money than the country can afford to have in circulation.

Stop banks and other financial institutions from lending so much money.

Questions

1 How is inflation measured?   2
2 Why is inflation 'a bad thing'?   4
3 What three ways are suggested as causes of inflation?   3
4 In what ways might the government try to cut inflation but not affect the amount of money people have to spend?   3
5 If the government cuts its own spending to try to cut inflation, what other problem is it creating? Why?   2
6 Using Table 11, which items have increased in price most? Which of the government solutions might help the shopper?   4
7 Using the graph at the bottom of the page, what has happened to inflation in Britain since 1963? Have the government's attempts to check inflation been successful?   8
8 What efforts can an individual make to reduce the effect of inflation on him/herself?   3

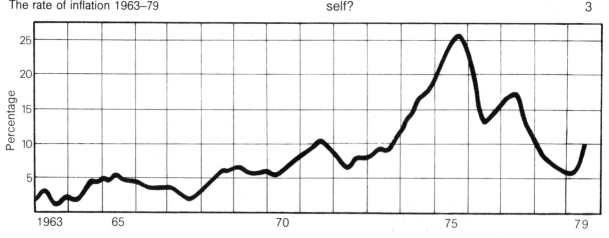

The Balance of Payments

The balance of payments of a country is the difference between the cost of everything it buys from abroad (imports) and the cost of everything it sells abroad (exports). If we pay more for foreign goods and services than we receive from abroad for our goods and services we will have a balance of payments deficit. If, on the other hand, we export more than we import, we will have a balance of payments surplus.

Just as an individual wants his or her bank account to be 'in the black' rather than 'in the red', so any country will want to be in surplus, and it is the duty of a government to encourage people to create a surplus.

THE EFFECT OF A DEFICIT

If a country spends less than it earns, then all is well; if a country spends more than it earns, then it is in danger of bankruptcy.

Britain is traditionally a trading nation. We do not have sufficient quantity or variety of raw materials (including food) to support ourselves, so we have to import them, usually in exchange for manufactured goods and services such as insurance and shipping.

If Britain expects to be able to sell goods and services to other countries, then they expect to be able to sell us goods and services in return, especially if they are cheaper or better than those which we can provide for our own people.

UK Balance of Payments 1970–78

Surplus in million £s +

1500
1000
500
0 — 1970 1971 1972 — 1973 1974 1975 1976 — 1977 1978
500
1000
1500
2000
2500
3000
3500

Deficit in million £s —

Other countries have more confidence in a country which can pay its way. If a country is in deficit for a long time, it has to borrow money in order to pay for essential raw materials which can be turned into manufactured goods for sale. Other countries or banks charge high interest rates or impose strict conditions for such loans.

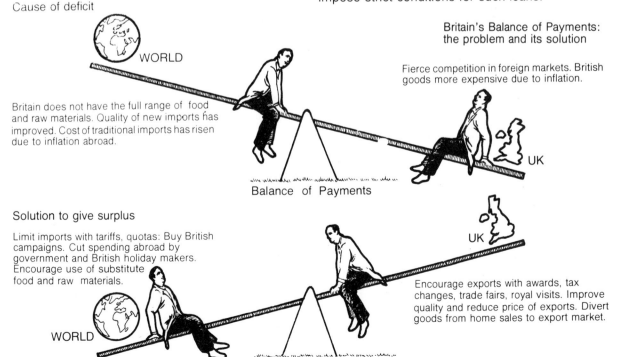

Cause of deficit

WORLD

Britain does not have the full range of food and raw materials. Quality of new imports has improved. Cost of traditional imports has risen due to inflation abroad.

Balance of Payments

Britain's Balance of Payments: the problem and its solution

Fierce competition in foreign markets. British goods more expensive due to inflation.

UK

Solution to give surplus

Limit imports with tariffs, quotas: Buy British campaigns. Cut spending abroad by government and British holiday makers. Encourage use of substitute food and raw materials.

WORLD

UK

Encourage exports with awards, tax changes, trade fairs, royal visits. Improve quality and reduce price of exports. Divert goods from home sales to export market.

Balance of Payments

Britain's problem, briefly stated, is that it imports too much from the rest of the world and exports too little to it.

The solution therefore, is to import less and export more.

Questions

1 Explain what is meant by a country being 'in the red'.   4
2. Why does a country try to have a balance of payments surplus?   4
3 What causes Britain to have a deficit?   3
4 How can Britain try to get a surplus?   3
5 Describe Britain's balance of payments record from 1970.   4
6 What effect might a government's attempts to solve a balance of payments problem have on an individual?   5
7 What efforts can an individual make to help Britain improve its balance of payments situation?   4

Growth

The government of every country wants its economy to secure greater wealth and a higher standard of living for its citizens. Improvement in these is measured by calculating the Gross National Product (GNP) – the total value of all that is produced by the country concerned.

The aim is not only to have a high rate of growth, however. Experience has shown that when there is a period of fast growth (a boom) it tends to be followed by a period of stagnation (a slump) during which there is either no rise in the standard of living or an increase which is based on borrowed or printed money, neither of which is desirable. Since these booms and slumps lead to uncertainty for the future, governments aim for a steady annual growth rate.

The achievement of a high and steady rate of growth in the economy can be hindered by:

Other Difficulties in the Economy
a) Inflation – a high rate of inflation may mean a reduction in demand for goods at home and may also make our exports less competitive.
b) Balance of Payments – a deficit may mean that foreign goods are more popular in the home market, thus reducing the demand for home-produced goods. It also suggests that our exports are struggling to compete.

c) Unemployment – an increase in unemployment may mean that fewer goods are produced and that people have less money to spend.

Poor Investment
If there is no investment in the economy this means a reduced efficiency and competitiveness. It may be caused by fear of a poor return on investment, uncertain economic conditions, or simply the attraction of investment elsewhere. Insufficient investment can also hinder growth. If our competitors can produce, say, five units of their good for £5 and we can only produce five units of the same good if we invest £8, then our investment is less efficient and our competitors could have put our extra £3 to better use.

Low Productivity
If it takes more man-hours for our industry to produce a quantity of goods than our competitors, then growth will be more difficult to achieve.

STEERING THE ECONOMY

In many ways the economy of a country can be regarded as a ship which has to be steered on a safe course through many hazards. The levers below show the sorts of measures which recent British governments have tried.

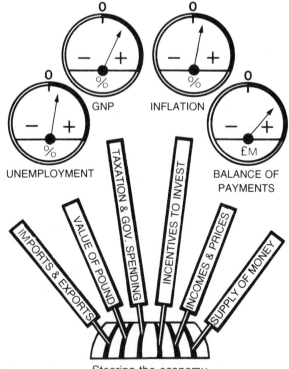

Steering the economy

A major problem is that while pulling a lever might correct an error in one dial, it might also cause another dial to move in the wrong direction. For example, if inflation is too high, the government might consider restricting wage increases, which might give people relatively less money to spend, which might result in higher unemployment. Or, the GNP might be raised by paying people higher wages, which results in inflation.

Moreover, when a government takes an economic decision it may also have political consequences, making the government more or less popular with the electorate.

Check for yourself how the economy works. Suppose that prices are rising too fast. Decide which of the levers to pull in which direction. Now check each of the dials to see what effect this measure has had on them. If they have moved, consider which lever to pull next.

By trying various solutions to various problem dials, you may begin to realise why steering the economy is not an easy task.

Questions

1 Why does a government want its country's economy to grow?   3
2 How is an economy's growth measured?   1
3 What is happening to an economy if it is described as having 'booms and slumps'?   3
4 Why do governments find it difficult to achieve a high and steady rate of growth?   6

Government spending on pensions, benefits, roads, schools, health, housing, defence

Government action on jobs, wages, prices, tax, VAT, interest rates, savings, hire purchase

Imports, exports, EEC, world prices, exchange rates, holidays abroad

How the problems of the economy affect the individual

Industrial Relations

Trade Unions

A Trade Union is a group of workers who have joined together to look after their own interests. Over forty per cent of people employed in Britain find it worthwhile to join a union.

Reasons for joining a union

To be able to **negotiate** the best possible conditions in one's workplace, e.g. holidays with pay, shorter working hours, bonuses, overtime pay, safety regulations, higher basic wages.

For job security. Control of apprenticeships and new entrants to the trade, as well as consultation over redundancy may prevent unemployment of members.

To prevent victimisation of individual members. This is achieved by 'strength through unity' or safety in numbers.

To ensure benefits for workers who are not at work because of sickness, injury, age or strike action.

To get equal pay for women workers, maternity leave, etc.

To negotiate adequate training for members through night school, evening classes, day release, etc.

To provide legal backing and advice for members.

To have some political power.

Reasons for not joining a union

Many better-off workers consider union membership unnecessary.

Some workers are in industries which are hard to organise, e.g. shop workers.

Some workers do not need the protection of a union, e.g. the self-employed, workers in small-scale firms who can speak to a sympathetic owner.

It is possible to get some of the advantages of union membership without actually joining, e.g. union-negotiated wage rises are given to all.

Some employers refuse to recognise or deal with unions.

Some people have conscientious objections to the principle of unionism.

Number of unions in the UK 1920–79

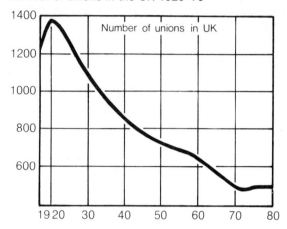

Total union membership 1920–79

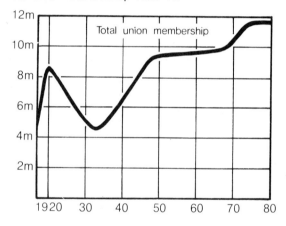

TYPES OF UNION

Craft unions are the oldest and smallest unions. Members are skilled craftsmen, e.g. musicians or locomotive drivers (ASLEF). Membership may fall as the skill dies out.

Industrial unions have a very strong position when they represent most or all of the workers in an industry, e.g. miners (NUM). Negotiations with employers may be easier as the union has previously settled its claims for different kinds of workers internally.

General unions take members from a variety of occupations, which sometimes makes it difficult to represent the differing interests of members. They have many unskilled members, e.g. TGWU and GMWU.

White-collar unions: for office workers, professional people, government officials, clerical workers, are the fastest-growing type of union. Until recently many of their members did not consider unions to be helpful to people in their position, e.g. USDAW and ASTMS.

HOW A UNION IS RUN

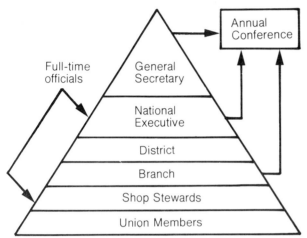

Membership From a total population in Britain of 56 million, 24 million are in full-time employment. Of these, 12 million are members of a trade union (8.5 million men, 3.5 million women). Some are deeply involved in their union's activities, many pay their dues and nothing more.

Shop Stewards A shop steward is usually the first person a member has contact with. They are unpaid, and elected by fellow members. Their duties may include recruitment of new members, collection of dues, checking on working and safety conditions, providing a link between union officials and members, conveying the views of workers to management and negotiating on behalf of members in the local workplace.

Branch The Branch is the basic unit in the structure of a union. It admits new members, elects delegates to attend union conferences, discusses and approves wage agreements, and organises union affairs in the area. The District controls the running of branches in the area.

National Executive These are the recognised leaders of the union. They are elected by the members and are responsible for national wage negotiations. They call for the beginning or end of official industrial action.

General Secretary The General Secretary is a full-time official, usually elected for life. He or she is involved in day to day running of the union on a national level, including national negotiations with employers, and is the spokesperson for the union to the media and the government.

Full-time Officials They try to help the shop steward in the day to day running of union business. They are skilled negotiators, are sometimes elected to the job, but do not earn a high salary.

Annual Conference Branches send delegates to represent them every year (usually at a seaside resort). Major policy decisions are then made after debates on motions presented by branches or by the National Executive. Voting is usually on a 'card vote'. Other decisions are taken during the year by the National Executive on the basis of assumptions of ordinary members' wishes, or after a ballot.

The role of the shop steward

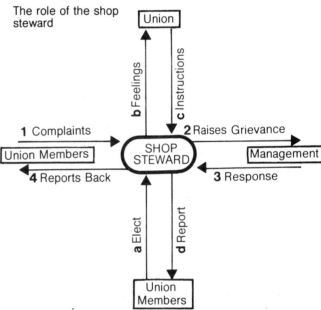

TRADES UNION CONGRESS

The TUC is the centre of the trade union movement in Britain: ninety-two per cent of all trade unionists in Britain belong to unions affiliated or linked to the TUC. It aims to improve the economic and social conditions of working people and deals with trade union issues nationally and internationally.

The annual congress is held every September. At this meeting a General Council is elected. It carries out congress decisions and gives the government the trade union viewpoint on economic, social and industrial issues.

Table 12 International comparison of industrial disputes days lost per 1000 employees (figures are for mining, manufacturing, construction and transport industries only) (*Dept. of Employment Gazette*)

Country	1970	1973	1976	1977*	1968–76 average
Canada	2190	1660	2270	820	1893
France	180	330	420	260	308
India	1440	1330	n.a.	n.a.	1369
Italy	1730	2470	2200	1480	1914
Japan	200	210	150	70	241
Netherlands	140	330	10	140	76
Sweden	40	10	10	20	41
UK	740	570	300	840	850
USA	2210	750	1190	n.a.	1340
W Germany	10	40	40	5	53

* provisional figures

The Scottish Trades Union Congress is the Scottish regional TUC and co-ordinates the activities of trade unions in Scotland and keeps them informed of national decisions.

There is a liaison committee between the TUC and the Labour Party which discusses policies on industrial relations and the problems of the economy. This committee was responsible for the 'Social Contract' agreement, part of the Labour government's action on prices and incomes from 1974.

The General Secretary of the TUC is in some ways a spokesman for all workers, just as the leader of the Confederation of British Industry (the employers' version of the TUC) is the spokesman for all managers.

Table 13 Stoppages of work due to industrial disputes in Britain (1973–6) (includes workers indirectly involved) (*Dept. of Employment Gazette*)

Number of working days lost per 1000 employees				
Industry	1974	1975	1976	1977
Agriculture/forestry/ fishing	55	—	—	5
Coal mining	18 800	175	225	300
Food industries	1 775	225	180	2 950
Chemicals	225	750	80	1 000
Iron and steel	1 550	750	750	1 500
Light engineering	2 950	2 125	850	2 900
Shipbuilding	3 750	2 750	325	900
Motor vehicles	3 550	1 800	1 750	5 500
Construction industry	200	200	425	230
Gas/electricity/water	175	30	150	240
Distributive trades	40	25	5	35
Insurance/banking/ business services	5	—	5	5
Total all industries and services	650	275	150	450

	EMPLOYERS	EMPLOYEES
SIDES AND SUPPORTERS	shareholders management board of directors Confederation of British Industry	workers shop stewards trade union officials Trades Union Congress
	Labour Party Conservative Party	
AIMS	lower costs higher profits greater output increased efficiency	higher wages better conditions shorter hours fringe benefits
	productivity	
WEAPONS (threat or action)	lock out redundancy lay-offs overtime ban strikebreakers	strike work to rule work-in overtime ban picketing

Collective Bargaining

Dispute at Brightlite

Brightlite make electric light bulbs for home use and for many other industries. They sell to supermarkets, the car industry, toymakers and fridge manufacturers. They have several factories, each making one type of bulb.

For many years they have had little trouble with industrial relations. There is only one union involved in their factories and communications between workers and their union and the management have been good until now.

Inflation has made prices rise sharply and the workers are complaining that their take-home pay is not high enough. They are asking for a thirty-five per cent pay rise. When the shop steward told the management representative of this, he was told there was no way the management could meet this demand. The union shop steward contacted his union headquarters and had some full-time officials visit the factory to talk to the management on behalf of the workers.

The shop steward is reporting on this meeting to the union at the end of the lunch break.

Phil This meat's like rubber. For the price we pay you'd think we'd get better than this. What's your fish like, Tam?

Tam No bad. Chips are rubbish, though. Shush. Here's the shop steward. I want to know what happened this morning.

Shop Steward Right lads, let's call the meeting to order. We have a problem here. You know the bosses wouldn't listen to me when I tried to get an extra thirty-five per cent for you, so I asked the **collective bargaining** experts to talk to them. Well, our full-time officials have been negotiating for us with the management . . .

Tam Did we get the money?

Shop Steward Patience, brother. They've offered us ten per cent. So what I have to ask you is: do you accept the management's offer or do we keep on pushing for thirty-five per cent? Do you want to think about it or will we go straight to a vote?

Members Vote! Vote!

Shop Steward OK. All those for ten per cent raise your hands. (Counts the few hands.) Thank you. Now all those in favour of sticking to our original demand for thirty-five per cent please show. (Counts many more hands.)

Members We're with you Bob!

Shop Steward Now, this means we will have to take some kind of industrial action to show the bosses we mean business. I'll tell you what the choices are and we can vote on it. First, we could keep talking to the management maybe with a conciliator to keep us talking?

Members No! No!

Shop Steward OK. The management obviously aren't going to offer us any more so we might ask someone to arbitrate for us.

Tam What's that?

Shop Steward Arbitrate? We call in someone who isn't involved and who is trusted by both sides to give a fair decision. We agree to stick to what he decides.

Phil Like a referee or umpire? Ah'm no having that, ah've seen some terrible referees in my time.

Shop Steward You may be right, Phil, and anyway, we should show them we're serious. We could have a work-to-rule where we only do what we are supposed to do and no extras.

Tam Like the railway guards checking all the doors on the train at every station? Holding up all the other trains?

Shop Steward Yes, and we still get paid. Maybe it's not drastic enough?

Tam We could always have a go-slow. Do the usual job only take ages to do it.

Shop Steward Can you go any slower, Tam?

Phil I think we should occupy the factory. Like the UCS folk did. Have a sit in, but keep working as well, and try to shame the management into giving in. We'd get publicity from the television.

Shop Steward That might work. Certainly we can't have an overtime ban since we don't have overtime. So it's either a work-in, or what I thought someone would have suggested long ago – a strike – a withdrawal of labour. We could either do it right away and . . .

Phil You mean a wildcat strike?

Shop Steward Yes. Catch the management off their guard. Mind you, we want our union to agree, so that it's official. If it's unofficial we don't get strike pay from the union or their backing. Are you ready to vote? Strike, work in, work to rule, keep talking or what?

As the shop steward said at the beginning of the meeting, 'We have a problem here.' In fact, there are several problems.

To start with it looks as though there is little communication between the workers and management in the factory, otherwise the dispute might have been settled without having to involve full-time officials. The management might have offered to improve conditions of work (like the canteen and the price of food) even if they could not offer more money.

The fact that the workers are thinking of taking industrial action shows that negotiations are not going well – perhaps the people involved are not very experienced negotiators. Or each side may feel it will lose face if it gives in to the other's demands. Often the people involved have an image of the other side which makes it difficult for them to see the other's point of view. For example, the workers may imagine the managers to be wealthy, money-grabbers who don't care what happens to their workers, while the management think the workers do very little work and only want to cause trouble.

Often, restrictions are put on free collective bargaining – negotiations between management and union with no interference. The government may have passed laws to regulate collective bargaining, or it may have placed a limit of some sort on the wage rises which can be offered.

The effects of industrial action are wide-ranging. A strike will mean that the workers lose money, the management and the firm will lose money and probably future orders too. Other factories which use the factory's products may have to lay off workers if they are short of light bulbs. The workers' families will also suffer. If it is an official strike they will get some money as strike pay from the union, but if it is unofficial they will only receive Supplementary Benefit. Obviously families paying mortgages or hire-purchase payments as well as food and fuel bills will be badly affected and have to spend their savings. But the effects of industrial action are wider. The whole country is damaged – less is produced so less is sold, perhaps for export. Our reputation abroad suffers: foreigners will be less likely to place orders with British companies if they think the firm is likely to have a strike and so delay delivery.

The management of Brightlite hold a meeting to discuss the dispute and the threat of industrial action.

Chairman of the Board How did your meeting with the union go, James?

James Not very well, I'm afraid, sir. They are insisting on thirty-five per cent. I tried to explain to them that we just do not have that sort of money, and anyway the government have said no-one should get more than fifteen per cent. But they said other firms were managing better deals than we were offering and started talking about industrial action . . .

Chairman The last thing we want is industrial action of any type. Even a work to rule would cut our production rate and lose us orders.

James Can't we just give them twenty per cent. They started talking about our works across the town and how they were thinking of holding a joint meeting.

Manager No! We certainly can't give them more than the government limit. You know what they did to Jones down the road. No more government contracts, no more government grants. We can't afford that. We'll just have to try harder here and alert our other factories so that a joint deal is worked out, before they send out the pickets.

Chairman I suppose if things really reach deadlock we could contact the Advisory, Conciliation and Arbitration Service. They did an excellent job for McBride's Engineering – came to a decision which suited both sides, and no working time lost. I think it is because ACAS are independent.

Manager That is a bit drastic. Surely there's more talking that can be done. What about offering as much money as possible and some worker participation in running the firm . . . say a seat on the board for one of the men?

James Yes, I think they would jump at that. The union has been on at me for some time about doing something about the Bullock Report on Worker Participation.

Chairman That's the first I've heard of it. Really, James, it is your job to negotiate with the union and tell us what they are thinking so that we can avoid trouble. If you had done your job properly we might not be in this situation now.

Letters to the Glenforth Courier

Dear Sir,

Once again the workers are not working. It's the unions to blame again. They don't need an excuse to go on strike these days. Not enough money they say. How would they like to live on a pension, that's what I would like to know.

The unions have too much say in the running of the country for my liking. They can hold the management of a good firm like Brightlite to ransom just because they are greedy for money.

It's time the government did something about it. Why not make strikes illegal and put the lot of them in jail? Get the workers working for a change. I know for a fact that all the men at Brightlite want to do the night shift because they can sleep all the time.

Yours, Fred Hamilton

Dear Sir,

My husband is one of the workers at Brightlite, and is involved in the dispute. I was really angry when I read Mr Hamilton's letter and would like to reply to some of his comments.

First of all, the workers at Brightlite want a rise because, compared with other industrial workers in the town they are poorly paid and work in poor conditions. I'm sure Mr Hamilton would not like to work in the noise of the factory or eat in the canteen there.

If the unions were not there, bad managers could do what they liked – pay the men very little, hire and fire workers when they liked. Workers have to thank the unions for the good working conditions most of them have today.

Perhaps if the managers and people like Mr Hamilton thought a bit more carefully about what it is like to work in a factory all the time they wouldn't say silly things like 'make strikes illegal' and spread nasty rumours like 'sleeping on the night shift'.

Yours, Judith Bennet (Mrs)

James Sorry, sir, I didn't think.
Manager No good apologising now, let's see if you've forgotten to tell us anything else. It's not a political strike is it? Not set up by someone to get publicity for someone or something? You haven't dismissed a worker for not wearing a tie and are going to tell us we'll be up before an Industrial Tribunal?
James No, nothing else. Just about money . . . and conditions too.
Chairman What conditions?
James The canteen is . . . Well, sir, would you eat there?
Manager There are laws, though. The place is clean and no one gets ill.
James But there are no laws about tough meat, and dull menus. The price, too, is a bit steep – especially since there's nowhere else for them to eat.
Chairman We might have an answer here, now let's just . . .

It looks as though the dispute at Brightlite is nearly over. The management has found what looks like being a solution to the problem – an improved canteen and as much money as they can offer.

In the future, though, James will have to be trained to carry out his job as negotiator in a more skilled way and to inform his colleagues of progress and problems. The appointment of a worker to the Board of Directors might help communications and iron out problems in the future if, say, a new machine were to be introduced. Management would be aware of the problems it might create before the introduction, if their worker board member is involved in early discussions.

They are lucky that, at least so far, the Press, radio and television have not spotlighted the dispute. Usually the publicity gained does no harm, but sometimes the story is distorted and side issues become more important than the main cause of the dispute.

Nurses picket outside Greenwich Hospital, 1978

Laws and Government Action

LAWS ABOUT INDUSTRIAL RELATIONS

In 1967, a **Royal Commission on Industrial Relations** (the Donovan Report) examined current problems in industrial relations and recommended changes, including greater recognition of the importance of the shop steward. In 1969 the Labour government introduced a White Paper called 'In Place of Strife'. It proposed legislation which would, it claimed, give benefits to both sides of industry. However, trade union pressure forced the withdrawal of the planned legislation.

In 1971, the **Industrial Relations Act** was a Conservative Government attempt to make collective agreements binding by law; to supervise trade union rules; define unfair industrial practices like the closed shop and impose a sixty day 'cooling-off' period and a ballot of union members before a strike. This act was repealed by the Labour Government in 1974.

In 1974, the **Trade Union and Labour Relations Act** and its 1976 amendment made collective agreements no longer legally binding; gave immunity to peaceful picketing and set out legal requirements and status for trade unions and employers' associations.

In 1977, the **Bullock Report** recommended more industrial democracy and worker-directors to influence decisions on an equal basis with shareholders.

ACTION TO DO WITH CONDITIONS OF WORK

In 1970, the **Equal Pay Act** was an attempt to end wage **discrimination** against women, where the work being performed by men and women was the same or broadly similar.

In 1974, the **Health and Safety at Work Act** brought together many previous acts and widened them to cover everyone at work, and the general public. It also set up a commission to approve codes of practice agreed between employers and employees.

In 1975, the **Employment Protection Act** set up the Advisory Conciliation and Arbitration Service – an independent body to help in collective bargaining. The act also provided some security of employment for individuals and made rulings on unfair dismissal.

1975, the **Equal Opportunity Act,** backed by the Equal Opportunities Commission, attempted to end sex discrimination in employment opportunities.

ACTION ON PRICES AND INCOMES

Governments often want to be able to control the rate of increase of wages and prices. Workers ask for higher wages partly to keep pace with price increases and this in turn increases prices in an upward spiral. Some of these attempts have been 'statutory' – legally binding – others have been 'voluntary' – a matter of agreement between government, unions and employers. Each government has its own special labels for what it does, although it may be exactly the same as a previous government's attempts, e.g. freeze/standstill/pause.

1961–63 Conservative Unions were asked to hold back wage claims for six months and then to keep them below a norm of around three-and-a-half per cent. This was unsuccessful.

1966–70 Labour A statutory body, the Prices and Incomes Board had to approve increases. At first there was a 'standstill', then 'severe restraint', then a three-and-a-half per cent 'criteria'. The policy collapsed under increasing pressure from all sides.

1972–74 Conservative Another phased approach. It began with a 'standstill', then a limit of £1 plus four per cent, then seven per cent plus a 'threshold' based on the cost of living. It was enforced by a Pay Board and a Prices Commission but was defeated by the miners' strike, the introduction of the three-day week and the General Election which removed the Conservatives and put a minority Labour Government in power.

1974–79 Labour A voluntary policy was agreed with the TUC. It began with the 'Social Contract' which allowed wage increases to match the rising cost of living in return for promises of government action in other areas, such as old age pensions. Then followed a series of phases. Phase 1 was a £6 per week upper limit which was enforced with reserve legal powers. Phase 2 was a four-and-a-half per cent 'restraint' plus tax concessions from the chancellor. Phase 3 asked for a ten per cent 'guideline' with a promise of further tax cuts if inflation fell below ten per cent a year. This was enforced, by and large, in the public sector and the government also showed that they were prepared to penalise firms in the private sector who went above the guideline. Phase 4 asked for a guidline of five per cent.

Questions

1 Using the introduction to Brightlite and the section on employers and employees, what would the aims of management and workers in this factory be?   3
2 What reasons might the workers give for wanting a thirty-five per cent rise?   2
3 What could they do to try to get what they wanted?   3
4 What can the management do to try to get what they want?   3
5 Who will suffer if there is a stoppage at Brightlite?   4
6 What had James, the management's negotiator, done which made the dispute more difficult to solve?   2
7 What settlement might be reached between the management and workers at Brightlite?   3
8 How might the government have helped them reach a settlement?   3
9 What view do the general public often have of workers taking industrial action? Why might they have this view?   3
10 In what ways has the government tried to ensure less trouble in industrial relations?   5
11 In what ways has the government tried to ensure that all workers have good working conditions?   3
12 What legislation is there to do with the rights of women who work? Why was this legislation needed?   5
13 Why does the government want to control prices and incomes?   2
14 Describe the most recent policy on Prices and Incomes.   3

Workers vote on a managerial decision, Upper Clyde Shipbuilders

PART 3

Society

Living in Scotland

Introduction

At various times in their lives people have to make decisions about how and where to live. They must ask themselves certain questions and their different answers result in many different life styles.

Where to live? In town or country; in the Highlands, Central Belt or Borders; in a flat or a house?

How to earn money? Working indoors or outdoors; self employed or wage earner; a career or part time?

What to do with the money? Spend or save?

People are very rarely able to make a completely free choice but have to take into account various limiting factors. And all the time the government and other organisations are engaged in offering advice, giving assistance, encouraging certain decisions and preventing others.

Because of this individuals become communities and communities make up society.

Industrial Base

The late 18th century saw the Industrial Revolution in Scotland. The growth of factories led to a rapid increase in population in the Central Belt and in industrial towns elsewhere. To cope with the incoming workers, most towns quickly built standard tenement houses which had basic sanitary provisions for the time. Later, these houses, though sturdy, neared the end of their useful lives and fell well below the accepted standards of sanitation. Today, they form the slum areas of the big cities.

At the same time, the demands on industry were changing. The power used changed from coal and steam to gas and electricity, making the siting of factories less dependent on coalfields. Manufacturers preferred to site their factories nearer the

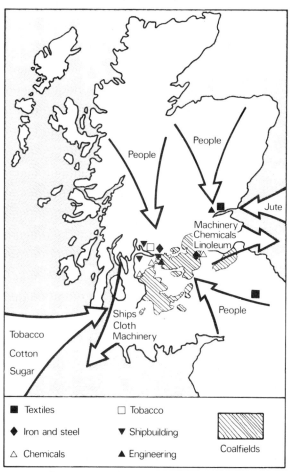

■ Textiles	□ Tobacco	
♦ Iron and steel	▼ Shipbuilding	Coalfields
△ Chemicals	▲ Engineering	

Scotland's traditional industrial base

markets, which were mainly in the Midlands and South-east of England. When the traditional heavy industries of coal, steel, shipbuilding and textiles began to decline, Scotland was badly hit. The newer industries: consumer goods, light engineering and science-based industries, all established themselves near markets in the south, where the **infrastructure** of transport, administration, etc. was more favourable than in the north.

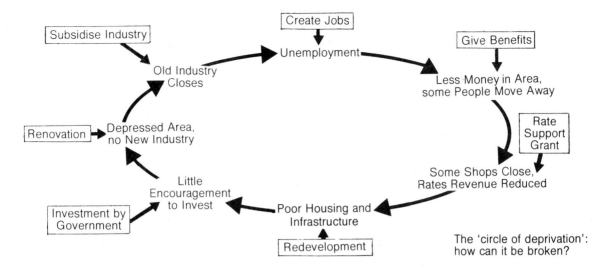

The 'circle of deprivation': how can it be broken?

It became government policy to encourage new industries and other sources of employment to move to areas where industries were declining and unemployment was high (most of Scotland as well as Northern Ireland, Wales and Northern England). Chrysler at Linwood and BLMC at Bathgate were discouraged from setting up in the South; an aluminium smelter and paper-making factory were established at Fort William with the attraction of abundant hydro-electric power; the proposed major steelworks at Hunterston will have an adjacent ore terminal and electricity supply from the nuclear power station; government offices were directed north, such as the National Savings Bank in Glasgow and Inland Revenue at East Kilbride; the Ministry of Defence is to set up in the St Enoch Square area of Glasgow; many firms have established branch factories in Scotland, often on industrial estates. The discovery of North Sea oil has given a further boost to the economy and many oil-related industries have been set up, especially in the east of Scotland.

The future of Scotland's industry, and therefore livelihood, depends on answers to the following questions:

Will firms close branch factories if times are hard?
Will future governments offer incentives to industry to move to 'areas for expansion'?
How long will North Sea oil last, and will we take full advantage of its potential benefits?
Can Scotland successfully break free from the circle of deprivation it has inherited from the past?

Deprivation occurs when an area suffers from several problems at once – housing problems, industrial problems, social problems, money problems. It can be shown as a circle. Start at any point on the circle and see how things get worse and worse. Then try to work out how the government or anyone else can break the circle – the circle of deprivation.

If the governing authorities do nothing, the area decays and the people remaining live in poverty. At each point, there are efforts which the government can and/or could make.

Probably the most ambitious action the government can take is to redevelop part of the decaying area. This involves knocking down most of the buildings in the area (except some of special interest or value, like historic buildings or hospitals) and rebuilding a complete area including factories, schools, shops, houses and roads to modern standards. This has been done in most big cities in Britain, and the changes can be quite dramatic. In Glasgow, the Eastern Area Renewal Project is using money from the Local Authority, the Scottish Development Agency, the Scottish Special Housing Association, and the Urban Aid Programme to do this. Local people are asked to comment on proposals and make suggestions to the planners at special meetings. The worst areas are to be demolished; many houses are being modernised or rehabilitated; advance factories are being built to attract industry and special small-scale factory units are being built. New sports facilities are planned and considerable landscape improvement underway. This large scale plan includes an attempt to avoid some of the shortcomings of earlier 'solutions' to deprived areas. People can stay in their local area; industry, as well as housing, is planned rather than haphazard; recreation **facilities** are included; local citizens are given the opportunity to air their views and become involved.

*Extract from article in
Glenforth Courier*

'It is indeed a sad day for Glenforth. The shipyard gates closed for the last time today at Young's as 1500 men walked home jobless, or redundant as they call it now. Only 200 of them have been promised jobs in the next town in McLay's yard. They said it was rationalisation – concentrating the work in the modern yard, where they are equipped to build bulk carriers instead of the famous Young's luxury liners which no one wants any more.

The impact of the yard closing will be felt far and wide. Many other local firms will be hit. Take for example the firm of McKinley and Thoms. Mr Thoms Junior said today, 'This is a blow for us. Who wants to buy our propellor shafts now with Young's gone. I doubt if my workforce will have a happy Christmas this year.'

Even local shopkeepers will suffer – those near the yard who supplied 'pieces' and soft drinks have already put up their shutters and moved. The manager of the big department store in town sees hard times ahead for his business. Who's going to buy a new three-piece suite and new clothes out of redundancy money and Social Security. Even the food shops can put away their exotic food – more bread and jam!

Many of the Campbells, McLarens and McKays whose ancestors came to Glenforth during the Highland Clearances are fed up living in Glenforth anyway. Mr Thomas Ure (60), said, 'I've lived here all my life, and it sickens me to see the changes around here. Time was you could walk the streets safely. Now you're scared to leave your house. And the houses – I remember when they were almost new and people were proud of them – wally closes and all. Now they're almost falling down and the facilities are rotten. One toilet for every three families and hot water out of a wee geyser. I wish I could move, but who would want to take me on?'

Certainly the scene is most depressing. Idle cranes above a dirty river; smoke from the one remaining factory pouring through filthy back courts; gang slogans written on anything that stands still; political slogans written on the roads promising a new world.

It looks as though many people will try to move away from Glenforth. Those with skills should be able to find work, perhaps in the oil boom areas or the New Towns. The semi- and unskilled will just have to hope for the best. Many of those who will leave are the backbone of the community – running clubs, organising the Gala week, and speaking up for the community to the council when things go wrong. But what will happen when they are gone? There are strong rumours that with fewer people living in the town and fewer children (it seems to be young families who move out) at least one of the schools will close. The local hospital too is threatened with reorganisation. One or two dentists and GPs have already gone. All this on top of the closure of the last cinema and Bingo hall, and only one café makes this a depressing place. Are streets of empty houses all we can hope for? The council says it no longer has the money coming in from the rates to pay for more than essential repairs. Unless a new industry moves in they cannot see things getting any better . . . and what industrialist would want to set up his business in a place with nothing to offer but its pride in a glorious past?'

Living Patterns

There are more than five million people living in Scotland. Not everyone lives in areas as deprived as 'Glenforth'. Not everyone lives in a city. The studies which follow show some of the 'living patterns' to be found in Scotland. They should give you an idea of how people live in parts of Scotland different from your own.

Hamish McDonald – a Crofter

Hamish rents a small five-acre croft in the Western Isles but, like other crofters, has security of tenure – he cannot lose the croft. It is part of a township of ten crofts on the shore. His four cows graze the common land on the edge of the township and his sheep are on the nearby hills. With the thin, poor soil and cool, wet weather, Hamish can't grow much – oats, potatoes and vegetables in a few small fields near the house. He makes some money from milk, wool and eggs and the occasional bullock which he sells, but if it wasn't for his weaving work and his wife doing bed and breakfast in the summer, they, like so many others, would have to give up the croft.

Some of the crofts are not worked now and have been taken over as holiday houses, others are badly neglected as the crofters are too old to work the land. Hamish's two children are the only ones in the township and he doesn't think they will stay to run the croft. After travelling to the mainland to secondary school and tasting the 'bright lights' of town life, not to mention the job opportunities, they are unlikely to want to spend the rest of their lives in the quiet township.

The government has tried to help the township – grants and loans are not too difficult to get to improve land or extend the house a bit to help with the tourist trade, but they can do nothing about the high cost of living in the islands and the remoteness of the place.

Ronnie Forbes – Super Salesman

Ronnie likes nothing better than a week's work based on his home town. He doesn't mind travelling from town to town selling soap powder, but he much prefers being able to come home every evening and put his feet up. He lives in a semi-detached house in an estate on the edge of a large city. After saving hard for several years, he and his wife managed to get a mortgage and buy their 'dream home' – it will be theirs in the year 2001!

Life on the estate is very pleasant. Most of the people are about Ronnie's age and, like him, have young families. That means his children have lots of others to play with in the large gardens and the local swing park and his wife has lots of friendly neighbours to go to the shopping centre with. There is usually one wife who can take the rest of them in the family car. His wife also helps with the estate playgroup where his youngest child goes two mornings a week.

His parents live in the centre of town which means they are not too close – a good thing Ronnie thinks. He goes to see them with the kids every couple of weekends – having a company car makes it all very simple. They usually go on holiday with them too – a package to somewhere sunny – grandparents make great babysitters!

Ronnie goes to the local hotel for a drink on a Friday night with some friends from the estate – mostly young professional people like himself – there's a policeman, a teacher, a shop manager and another salesman. In the summer they usually manage a few rounds of golf. Apart from their golf handicaps, they talk about the rising crime rate (shoplifting in particular), the 'youth of today', and the rival merits of different brands of soap powder.

A crofting community, South Uist

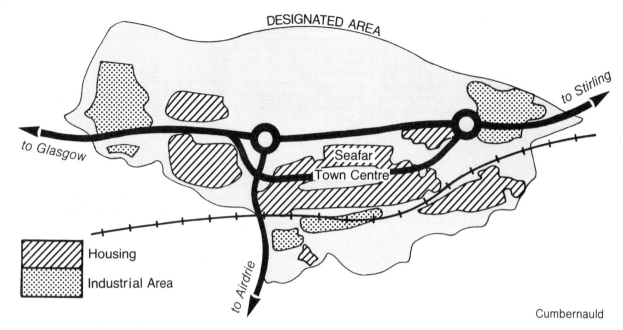

DESIGNATED AREA

to Stirling

to Glasgow

Seafar
Town Centre

to Airdrie

Housing

Industrial Area

Cumbernauld

Life in a Scottish New Town

Jimmy Paterson lives with his family in Seafar, Cumbernauld, in one of the modern single-aspect houses. It took the family some time to get used to living in a house with bedrooms downstairs and living room and kitchen on the first floor, but it certainly gave them pleasant views of the landscaped walkways and gardens and no one overlooked their house. Jimmy's wife likes the cul-de-sac style of community housing. She soon got to know the eight other families living in her cul-de-sac and it made settling in much easier — feeling part of a small community. She also likes the walkways — she can walk to the local shops or to the town centre without fear of the children running on to a road or into the path of cars. There are pedestrian footbridges across the main roads and traffic-free areas make it really safe for children. They also like the way the neighbour-hoods have small groups of shops, primary schools and medical services. The town centre provides them with big chain stores, banks and hotels and pubs for the occasional night out. The sports centre is a big favourite with Jimmy and his son. Everything in the town is just where it should be, according to Jimmy. Garages for private cars are near the houses, but the roads to them avoid the gardens, play areas and walkways. Different types and styles of houses are mixed together so that there is constant variety. The industrial estates are totally separate from the residential areas so there are no problems of noise or air pollution. Everyone can get to the town centre easily — on foot, by bus or by car.

Cumbernauld New Town

Urban–Rural Contrasts

	Rural (to do with villages, hamlets, isolated settlements)	Urban (to do with towns and cities)
Population	Small number of people living in small groups or isolated units. Small range of possible friends. Extended family is important.	Large number of people living close together. Wide choice of friends. 'Family' less important.
Housing	Single family houses, cottages of different ages. Owned or rented privately or may be tied to job. Gardens for vegetable growing and poultry common.	Large variety of house type and tenure. Much is local authority owned. Much is high density tower blocks or tenement flats. Gardens small and rare. Some allotments.
Education	Small one- or two-teacher village schools. Composite classes common. Secondary schooling means travelling long distance or staying away from home. Further education limited.	Local primary and secondary schools within walking distance. Usually modern and well equipped. Further education widely available.
Shopping	Village stores for most shopping. Mail order important. Mobile shops and banks necessary. Prices tend to be high. Have to go to market town for major purchases.	Local shopping centres for most shopping. Some mobile shops for housing schemes. Wide choice including cut-price supermarkets and discount stores. Near major shopping centre.
Social Services	Doctor will serve area but major surgery has to go to city hospital. Dentist at distance. Provide own care for old people, families with problems, etc.	Choice of doctors/dentists, often in modern group practices in health centres. Hospitals offer wide range of specialist services. Full range of social and welfare services available. Voluntary organisations run play groups, etc.
Job Opportunities	Limited, and mainly linked to agriculture, or services like shops, garages, post office.	Fairly wide choice. Factories. Opportunities to train or retrain. Competition for jobs.
Transport	Public services only between larger centres. Car almost essential.	Integrated transport service. Publicly operated rail and bus network. Air travel from larger centres.
Entertainment	Generated locally, e.g. choirs, drama groups, own family. Little 'canned' entertainment. TV, radio reception may be poor.	Wide range – cinemas, discos, dance halls, clubs, football matches, sports centres, swimming pools, concerts, TV, radio.
Environment	Fresh air, open space, quiet, generally pleasing.	Air pollution widespread, some parks, gardens, play spaces. Many areas very run down and dilapidated. Often depressing.
Crime and other social problems	Little crime or vandalism. Problems are solved by local community. Underemployment.	Crime rate high especially in bigger cities. Racial problems. Religious conflict. Broken homes, single-parent families. Delinquency fairly widespread. Unemployment.

Housing scheme – shops and houses

Mary Jamieson – Life in a Housing Scheme

'The house is fine, central heating, our own bathroom and quite big really. It's the place I don't like. There's street after street of houses and nothing else. Every street seems to look like every other one. Only a few folk bother with the gardens – kids run through them and they paint things on the walls. I don't blame them really – there is nothing for them to do – a swing park isn't much use to a teenager. Cinemas or dancing mean an expensive trip into town. There's one chip shop and one youth club for hundreds of kids. You'd think the council who build this place would have realised we needed more than just houses to live in. Fair enough, there's a big sports centre and a shopping centre opening in a year or two but I've been here ten years! And the people who planned this place never tried living in it with a family – they haven't stood in the rain for half-an-hour waiting for a bus to the shops with two toddlers and a pram. Nor have they thought about how much more expensive it is living out here on the edge of the town – bus fares cost a fortune, and there are so few shops they can charge what they like . . .'

Border Knitwear Factory Worker

Henry Scott worked for many years in a knitwear factory in the Borders. The factory produced woollen sweaters, waistcoats and dresses mainly for the British market. He was one of the few men who worked in the factory – it was mainly women's work. Last year the factory closed, but Henry had seen the end coming for a while. It could no longer compete with most of the other factories in the area, which produced the higher quality woollen and cashmere garments for which there was still a great demand – especially from overseas markets. Henry was glad to retire early, but for his younger male colleagues it would mean job hunting and even re-training. Many of them would find employment with one of the new industries – in particular, electronics and processing plants for the produce of the agricultural and fishing industries – that were coming to the Borders. Henry himself would make the most of his retirement, and continue to enjoy the rugby!

Questions

1 Describe Scotland's traditional industrial base. Mention industries, raw materials, labour force.   8
2 What type of houses were built for the workers who came into Central Scotland?   2
3 Outline the main economic problems which Scotland has had in the 1970s.   5
4 What social problems have resulted from these economic problems?   3
5 What solutions can you suggest for an individual caught up in the circle of deprivation?   4
6 Compare life in different parts of Scotland under these headings: housing, recreation, jobs, the future.   20
7 If you were asked to plan a new town from scratch, which of these would you plan in which order, and why? Houses, roads, factories, play areas, open spaces, schools, shops, entertainment.   5
8 What are the main differences between life in the countryside and life in large towns?   6

North Sea Oil and Gas

Datelist

1959	Natural gas found in Holland
1964	Continental Shelf Act divides up North Sea; licensing
1965	Licensing; gas in UK sector
1967	UK gas ashore
1968	Oil in Ekofisk field – Norwegian sector
1969–70	Licensing, oil in Forties field – British sector
1972	Licensing
1975	UK oil from Argyll field comes ashore by tanker; government takes majority share in fields discovered; BNOC set up
1976–7	Licensing; oil discovered in Moray Firth

The British sector of the North Sea is divided into blocks. The government issues licences giving exploration rights to oil companies. The British National Oil Corporation was set up in 1975 to control exploration, development, pipeline installation and refining, and to control the rate of depletion of the oil to ensure the greatest long-term benefit to Britain. The Offshore Supplies Office (under the Department of Energy) in Glasgow, gives advice and information to firms and encourages them to compete in overseas markets, 'Buy British', and to take advantage of financial assistance offered under the Industry Act and through EEC funds.

THE EFFECTS ON THE ECONOMY

The discovery of oil in the North Sea has made, and will continue to make, a great difference to the British economy. The boost given to oil-related industries for example has kept unemployment lower than it might otherwise have been.

The balance of payments has also benefited. In the past Britain had to import large amounts of crude oil amounting to about eighteen per cent of her total imports bill. This oil came from the Middle East, Algeria, Nigeria and Venezuela, and is no longer needed in such large quantities. Some oil still has to be imported, as North Sea oil is mainly light oil and has to be mixed with heavier imported oils.

The government has been concerned that the British people should benefit directly from the oil in the North Sea. Revenue has been raised from the oil companies not only in the form of the usual Corporation Tax on oil company profits (fifty-two per cent) but also from the Petroleum Revenue Tax on gross revenue, after allowances for capital spending on rigs, boats, etc. In 1978 the government decided that the existing rate of PRT of forty-five per cent was too generous and announced a rise to sixty per cent from January 1979.

Peterhead – Boom Town

Before the oil boom, Peterhead had a population of 14 000, a top security prison and a fishing industry, some ship repairing and a food-processing factory. Unemployment was high and many school leavers left to find jobs elsewhere.

The town has been transformed by oil and gas discoveries. The harbour made it ideal as a supply base for rigs and pipe-laying barges (one supplies eighty ships a week in summer, thirty in winter). A tanker terminal is being built in the bay to supply the new Boddam power station which opened in 1978.

Oil-related industries

Related to extracting oil
rig building
platform building
steel, supply-boat building
valve and pump making,
pipeline making and coating,
house building, diving equipment,
helicopters, food manufacture

Related to processing oil
refineries, tank farms,
chemical factories,
plastics, paints,
artificial fibres, fuels

Peterhead

The oil pipeline from the Forties field comes ashore at Cruden Bay, south of Peterhead. Gas from the Frigg field comes ashore at St Fergus, north of the town, where an ammonia plant is planned. The town was a base for much of the pipe-laying work.

There are branch offices of the big oil companies and offices of drilling companies, supply boat and construction companies in the town.

Apart from construction labour for projects like the tanker terminal, who come from all over Britain and live in workcamps, most of the labour is local, stemming the Peterhead 'brain drain'.

Wage rates have risen and as more people are staying in the town so have rents and house prices (a house costing £8000 elsewhere costs £15 000 in Peterhead). Shops are booming, and new ones opening selling luxury goods like cameras and hi-fi. The two hotels have had a new lease of life and the new community centre with swimming pool and sports hall is complete.

Not everyone welcomes the boom; many are worried about possible pollution from the terminal and ammonia plant. The fishing industry, in decline, has had increased costs of fuel, poor catches and workers leaving for steady shore jobs. The older people of the town are unhappy about the incomers, especially as they are all men, and are anxious that the old way of life does not end. Others are more concerned about the end of the oil boom and are pressing for diversification so that Peterhead does not suffer the same fate as towns which relied on construction yards and suffered badly during the famine of building in 1976–77.

The Rig Worker

Jim Henderson is a roustabout or general labourer on a drilling rig in the North Sea. He earns about £130 a week when he is working. His job is to unload materials from the supply boats, but often he is moved up to the drilling deck where the roughnecks change the drilling bits and fit in new lengths of piping as the drill works deeper. They need strength, real skill and split-second timing, and on the rigs you learn on the job. Jim can't refuse the American tool-pusher's instructions to take over from an injured roughneck – it is more than his job is worth – and he wants to move on to be a driller, watching the seabed on a television screen.

Accidents are common and as Jim knows a bit of first aid, he is called on to help the injured until the helicopter arrives from Aberdeen – an hour and a half's journey. With over a hundred men and many accidents Jim thought a doctor or at least a trained nurse would be essential. Better injured than washed overboard by twenty-metre waves. In winter the cold of the sea kills you instantly, in summer it numbs your legs in seven minutes.

Jim finds it a strain, too, not to be able to smoke during the twelve-hour shift and not to be allowed indoors except for the half-way meal break. That's one thing Jim likes – the food the Spanish cooks prepare is great. He also gets on better with them and the other Europeans in the crew than with the Americans, who have the better jobs.

Off-duty time is spent in a four-berth room, with a shower, or in the recreation room where films are

Changing a rock bit on a drilling platform 100 miles east of Shetland

shown. No alcohol is allowed. All the men look forward to their two weeks ashore after two weeks' work, if they can get off the rig. Jim remembers with horror the time his crew had to work for six weeks instead of two because the weather was too bad for the relief crew to be landed.

Jim usually goes home to his family in Edinburgh. Other men prefer to stay in Aberdeen in boarding houses and very quickly spend their working weeks' wages.

Jim is friendly with a bounce diver (one who decompresses between dives). Neither understand the saturation divers who work like astronauts from chambers under the sea and stay there for up to six weeks. The bounce divers get £40 a day and the saturation divers £60 – but this doesn't tempt Jim. Tales of the 'bends' and bone diseases, not to mention thirty deaths among a thousand divers in the North Sea put him right off. He might think about work in the construction yards though, less money, but steady work for a few years at least, and more amenities and unions.

WHOSE OIL?

We know that there is oil in the North Sea and that its discovery can bring many benefits to its owners. But what is less clear is *who* owns the oil.

Perhaps it belongs to Scotland. 'It's Scotland's Oil' says the SNP slogan – meaning the benefits of the discovery of oil near the coast of Scotland should go to the Scottish people.

Estimated offshore oil-production levels from the UK, 1975–85

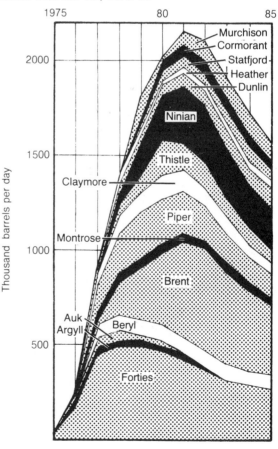

Perhaps it belongs to Britain because most of it lies in the British part of the continental shelf which is internationally agreed to be British. But who in Britain does it belong to?

Perhaps it belongs to the **government**, who run the country on behalf of the British people and should therefore have a say in who should benefit.

Perhaps it belongs to the British **taxpayer**, whose money has been used for exploration and development and who should now see a reduction in taxation to compensate for this.

Perhaps it belongs to our **creditors** – the countries and institutions who have lent money to us to tide us over economic crises until the oil came 'on tap'.

Perhaps it belongs to the **European Community**, since we are now members of that economic organisation.

Perhaps it belongs to the people who have done most of the exploration and development and are now extracting it – the **multi-national companies**, such as Shell, Esso and Texaco. They will expect a return on their investment in the vital resources of oil and natural gas.

Questions

1 Describe the way in which oil has been developed in the North Sea under these headings: exploration; drilling, transportation.   9

2 In what ways have oil towns benefited and suffered from the discovery of oil offshore?   6

3 When will the oil begin to run out and what can be done to prepare for this day?   3

4 What is life like for people on the rigs?   3

5 What special problems have to be faced by each of the following: oil rig workers; oil companies; government; suppliers to oil rigs?   8

6 Answer these questions, giving reasons:
  a) Whose oil is it?   3
  b) What short-term benefits will it bring?   3
  c) What long-term benefits could it bring?   3

North Sea oil and gas-fields

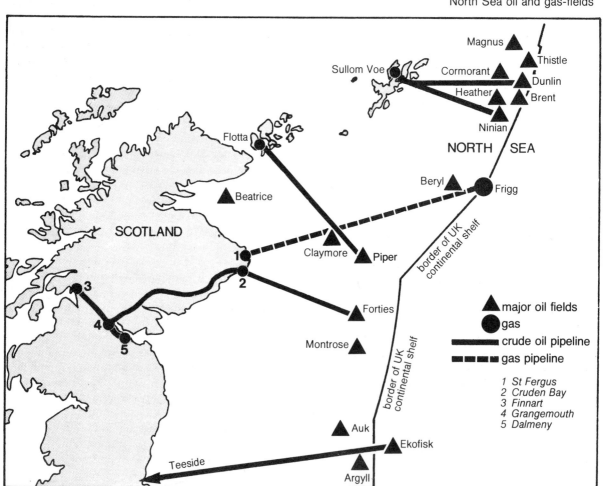

Work

Why work?

for food, clothing, shelter, luxuries

to have a position in society

because your job makes life better for others

for company

Getting a Job

Job opportunities depend on demand. For example, it will be harder to find a job in a declining industry, such as shipbuilding, than in an expanding or stable industry, such as petrochemicals. It will be easier to find a job in an area which is short of workers (e.g. Shetland) than in an area which is short of work (e.g. Strathclyde). It will be easier to find work in times of economic expansion than in times of recession. It will be easier to find work by looking in the right places for vacancies (e.g. newspapers, Job Centres, Youth Employment Offices, friends and relatives) rather than waiting for 'something to turn up'.

QUALIFICATIONS

There are two sorts of qualifications: certificates such as Ordinary or Higher Grades, school leaving certificates, university degrees, etc; and personal qualifications which are less easy to test — nimble fingers, neatness, colour sense, strength, literacy, numeracy, as well as personality factors such as patience, the ability to take or give instructions and initiative.

Most jobs require both sorts of qualifications. Both a brain surgeon and a transistor assembler will need nimble fingers and patience, though only the surgeon will also require a university degree. All workers need good health, though it is more important for a forestry worker to be in good health than someone who works indoors.

Some certificates are easier to get than others, because they are designed to show potential employers the different abilities of applicants for a job vacancy. Ordinary Grades are easier to pass than Higher Grades, which in turn are easier than university degrees. There are many other qualifications available, however, for those pre-

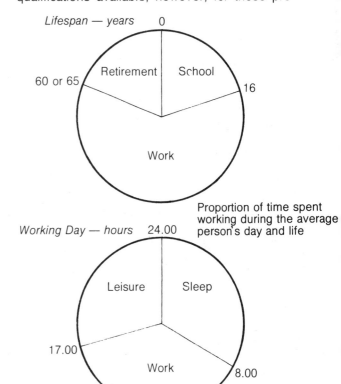

Proportion of time spent working during the average person's day and life

77

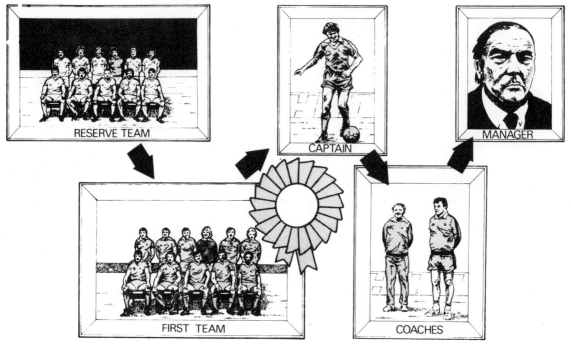

Work roles change with
increasing and changing skill

pared to study after they have left school. These
include City and Guilds certificates, courses at
technical college (perhaps on day-release from
work), Ordinary National Certificates or Diplomas
which provide training for many professional and
technical careers. Apart from these external
courses, much is learned on the job by
apprenticeships and the experience of work.

TYPES OF JOBS

Britain, being an advanced industrial nation, has a
vast range of jobs for people entering the labour
market to consider. The Industrial Revolution,
which brought division of labour and increased
specialisation, has made it more likely that people
will be required to settle into one line of work,
rather than be 'Jacks-of-all-trades'.

Jobs can be grouped in two different ways:
where the work is done – in a factory, office, shop
or outdoors;
the type of work involved – practical, intellectual,
social, physical.

The Potter

Bill is a craftsman potter. He works from his own
workshop in his back garden and sells his pots to
tourists and the local craft shop. Since he is his

Other Considerations

Job security?
Redundancy?

Health and safety
at work?
Discrimination?

Shop steward?
Trade Unions?

Training?
Promotion?

Wages?
Bonus?

Boredom?
Danger?
Dirt?

Right to work?

Social club?
Canteen?
Hairdressing?

Industrial injury
and disease?

Welfare?
Personnel Dept?

Factors affecting choice of work

own boss he can work when he feels like it and has no one telling him what to do. But he also has to make sure that his work is always of high quality – if it isn't it won't sell and he won't be able to eat or pay bills. Once he begins work he doesn't mind being on his own as company would distract him, but it can be lonely when he is just clearing up.

The 'Girl Friday'

Mary is the 'Girl Friday' for a fast-growing pop record firm. She never stops work from the minute she arrives until everyone else has gone home – whenever that is – she often works until late in the evening. She does all sorts of work – as a receptionist, typist, telephonist, pianist, model, signwriter, tea-maker, nurse – she does the lot and loves every minute of it, but because she feels part of the firm and involved in what it is trying to do, she doesn't mind working very hard. She is quite well paid and often gets expensive meals and trips to exciting places as part of the job.

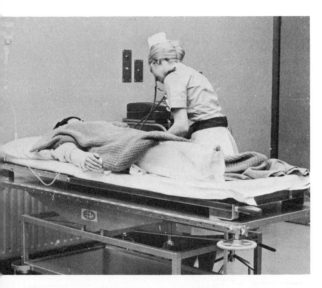

Work and the Law

The government offers assistance and protection to workers in a variety of ways.

Safety at Work

Health and Safety at Work Act (1974 and 1978) This extends previous legislation to everyone in any job (except domestic workers). Employers are liable to be sued for compensation if they do not ensure that workplaces are safe to work in. Representatives or committees of workers can review safety precautions.

Industrial Injuries Scheme Workers can claim Injury Benefit if they are off work for up to twenty-six weeks through an injury incurred at work. If they are disabled they may also claim Disablement Benefit, whether or not they have returned to work.

Equal Opportunity and Pay

Equal Pay Act (1970, enforced 1975) In 1970, employers were given five years to narrow the gap between men's and women's pay. The Act ensures that, with the backing of an Industrial Tribunal, where broadly similar work or work of equal value is being done by men and women, they will receive equal pay and fringe benefits (such as holiday entitlement).

Sex Discrimination Act (1975) This Act deals with discrimination in many areas, such as work, education and housing. The Equal Opportunities Commission and Industrial Tribunals ensure that, with the exception of some jobs, such as the armed forces, underground mining and competitive sports, men and women are not denied equal treatment in areas such as recruitment, advertisements, training, promotion, facilities, etc.

Race Relations Act (1976) strengthens the 1968 Act in ensuring that workers are not discriminated against on the grounds of race or colour. It covers the same areas as the Sex Discrimination Act and has a Commission for Racial Equality to uphold the terms of the Act.

Job Security and Unemployment

Contracts of Employment Act (1972); **Trade Union and Labour Relations Acts** (1974 and 1976); **Employment Protection Act** (1975) Employers have to be able to show to an Industrial Tribunal that

How much is a job worth:
Nurse – £?, Pop singer – £?

there was a genuine reason, such as misconduct or redundancy, for dismissal of a worker.

Workers can claim redundancy payment based on length of service, age and normal pay, if they are dismissed because of lack of work after two or more years in the job.

During unemployment, workers who have paid Class 1 National Insurance Contributions are entitled to Unemployment Benefit by Giro.

Employment Offices and Job Centres employ specially qualified staff to match those seeking work with those offering work. Free retraining courses are also on offer, and the Manpower Services Commission also gives help to young unemployed people by means of the Job Creation Scheme and the Youth Employment Programme.

It is often the trade unions who take the lead in ensuring that these Acts are enforced. It is now established that every worker has the right to join a trade union and that every worker and union can withdraw its labour (strike). ACAS exists to help where there is conflict.

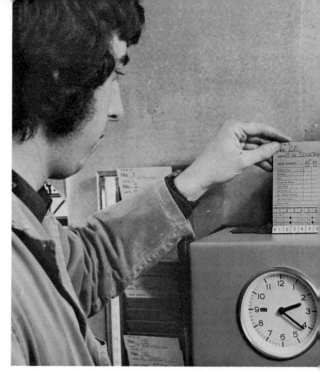

Clocking-in to work

The Industrial Tribunal

Helen worked as manageress in a large restaurant in a busy shopping centre. She was quite happy at her work until she discovered that the manager of another restaurant owned by the same firm was paid more money for doing what she thought was the same job. She became really upset when she realised that many of the waitresses under her were taking home more money than she was because of the tips they received

Helen contacted her union and was advised to put her case to her employers and see if she could be given the same wage as the manager she had heard about. She asked for and was granted an interview, but it didn't last long. 'You're a woman,' they said, 'you can't manage the waitresses as well as a man. And besides, what if you marry and start a family? You'll leave us and we'll need to train someone else.'

Helen went straight along from that interview to the Employment Office to complain. They gave her an application form for an appeal to the Industrial Tribunal.

At the hearing, Helen pointed out that she did the same work as the other manager, that she had worked for the firm longer than he had, and that the Equal Pay Act entitled her to the same wages. After asking the owners of the chain of restaurants some questions, the three men on the tribunal discussed the case briefly before giving their verdict. The member from the trade unionist panel was in no doubt. 'Exploitation of women – time it was stopped', he said. The employer member wanted to ask some questions about the waitresses but

was advised that this was not relevant in this case, since it only had to be decided whether Helen was doing broadly similar work to that of the man. The chairman, who was a lawyer, didn't even have to ask for a vote. They were unanimous in their agreement that the restaurant owners would have to pay Helen the same wages as the other manager.

The chairman was glad that this case was so straightforward – some of those he had to deal with concerning the Sex Discrimination Act, or the Employment Protection Act, among others, could be very complicated, especially if the other two on the tribunal disagreed and he had to decide with his casting vote.

Assembly Line

Peter answered an advertisement in the local paper for his job on the assembly line in an engineering works. He was attracted by the high pay which was offered and by the opportunities to work overtime, as the shift system had been abandoned.

His part in the production process is to attach a part to each engine that passes him and tighten a few nuts. At first he found it quite difficult to do the job quickly enough so that the line was not held up. But now the work comes automatically to him and he can let his mind wander to other things while his hands do the work almost by themselves. He can think about lunchtime when he will meet his mates in the subsidised canteen or about his game for the work's team on Saturday in the new recreation complex which the company built.

Any doubts about the monotony of the work were removed when he heard a rumour that the management were planning to retrain most of the semi-skilled workers to do different tasks if the unions could reach agreement on demarcation lines. His only worry is the threat of redundancy if the orders tail off, but then he would be entitled to enough benefits to tide him over any bad spell.

Signwriter

Hugh has been a signwriter for ten years. He was good at art at school and he felt he should try to find a job that used his skills. His uncle took him on as an apprentice and at first things were fine: good pay, regular hours, the satisfaction of a job well done.

Then things began to go sour. He felt lonely working on his own all day. His uncle wouldn't give him a pay rise when he had finished his apprenticeship and when the local steel mill closed down so did many of the businesses, like shops and offices, which used to give their orders to his uncle's firm. He would move away and try his luck in the big city, but his fiancée likes her job in a fashion boutique too much. He would find another job nearby but he isn't qualified for anything but writing signs. He would branch out on his own as an artist or something but he hasn't the capital or the nerve.

What now? The dole? Retraining? Or keep on at the same eyestraining job until his uncle retires and he inherits the firm?

Questions

1 What are the main reasons for working?   4
2 How large a part of people's lives is likely to be spent at work?   2
3 What considerations have to be taken into account before choosing a job?   6
4 Describe a football team as if it were a factory, from the unskilled workers to the manager, including items produced.   5
5 Who should be paid more – a pop singer or a nurse? Why?   4
6 Why do people sometimes have to 'clock in' at work and why do they sometimes rush out?   4
7 Describe likely problems at work if the government did not protect workers.   5
8 Describe what may happen if a worker feels he or she has been dismissed unfairly.   4
9 What are the advantages and disadvantages of each of the following jobs: potter; 'Girl Friday'; assembly line worker; signwriter?   8

Types of Pay

The basic pay which a person receives, before any extras are added or any deductions taken off, can be calculated in two ways: according to what he/she makes – piece rate – the more he/she makes, the more he/she is paid; or according to the time he/she works – time rate – this can be hourly, weekly or monthly.

There are various extras or bonuses that a worker can earn or be entitled to.

Increments are bonuses paid for each year of service. There are usually a limited number of increments before a worker reaches his maximum, e.g. young workers will get an increment each year until they reach adult wage, or teachers will get an increment each year until they reach maximum pay. These increments encourage workers to stay with a firm.

Commission is a bonus paid for making a sale. Often the basic pay is low, and workers can increase their take-home pay by working harder to make more sales and so earning more commission, e.g. car salesmen or shop assistants.

Overtime, usually time and a half or double time rate, is paid when some workers work outside normal working hours, e.g. Sunday.

Productivity bonuses are paid to workers who agree to change their way of working, perhaps by using a new machine and so increasing the amount they produce. During government incomes policy this is one of the few acceptable non-inflationary wage increases.

Promotion usually means a fairly large wage increase. Normally, the more skilled workers are promoted and rewarded for their extra responsibility and skill by an extra payment.

Merit payments cover a wide range of bonuses – from time-keeping to rewards for excellent work.

Fringe benefits include company cars, cheap mortgages, clothing allowances, discounts on company products, free insurance and luncheon vouchers. They can mean quite a lot to the worker – a car is 'worth' at least £600 a year to the worker who receives it – and are usually tax free and not usually affected by a government incomes policy.

Getting a Rise

Pay rises can come in many forms – flat rate, percentage increase, cost of living rise, bonus payments or fringe benefits.

Jim, a machine operator, and Peter, a manager, both work for the same firm and have been offered

What a typical pay slip means

Tax code Number given to worker by Inland Revenue to help them deduct tax correctly. It gives information on allowances due. Letter gives indication of status, i.e. married, single (L means single so lower allowances).

Basic pay Wages before any additions or deductions have been made.

Bonus Extra money for time-keeping, productivity, etc.

Overtime Extra money for working extra hours.

Gross pay Basic pay plus all additions.

Superann. Superannuation – usually a percentage of basic pay paid to pension fund.

Dues Trade union dues and contributions: may be paid directly by firm to union on member's behalf.

Nat. ins National Insurance contributions – earnings related, e.g. five per cent of earnings in most cases if the earner is an employee.

Savings Money deducted by employer to be paid into special savings scheme, e.g. holiday fund, Christmas club.

Net pay Wages after all deductions have been made – what you get 'in your hand'.

NAME	TAX CODE	BASIC PAY	BONUS	OVERTIME	GROSS PAY
YOUNG, F	097L				
	NAT INS NO	60·75	5·50	9·25	75·50
	AB112345A				

TAX	SUPERANN	UNION DUES	NAT. INS	SAVINGS	NET PAY
19·30	3·25	0·50	4·34	3·75	44·36

a variety of wage increases in a 'package deal'.

Last year both accepted a flat rate increase of £500. This brought Jim's wage up to £3000 and Peter's up to £10 000. Peter didn't think he really gained all that much from the £500 on top of the £9500 he was earning, but the extra £500 was a lot to Jim.

This year the firm has offered a 'package deal' of a percentage increase plus a number of other bonuses and benefits. Jim will gain £300 from the ten per cent increase but Peter will gain £1000 – a lot more. Because he is a low paid worker, and has a large family, Jim had been able to claim Family Income Supplement until he got this rise – now he is too highly paid to qualify for FIS or for other benefits, like free school meals – he thinks he is worse off than he was before the rise if he takes the lost welfare benefits into account (this is called the 'poverty trap'). Peter says most of his increase will go on tax.

The 'package deal' includes a cost of living rise – every time the Retail Price Index shows that the cost of living has risen more than one per cent, the workers will get a one per cent rise automatically.

Both men have been offered bonuses – Jim will get one if he agrees to use a new machine which will allow him to make more of the radio parts he welds together. This will be a productivity bonus because it will allow Jim to produce more parts in the same time. Peter has also been offered more money – an increment – because he has worked for the firm for more than a year and so the firm benefits from his experience.

Both get fringe benefits – Jim gets luncheon vouchers, free overalls and cheap travel to the factory in the work's bus. Peter gets a company car, a cheap mortgage and a big discount on any company product that he or his family want to buy.

Income Tax

Everyone who earns money is liable to pay income tax. In order to work out how much, a calculation is first made of how much income is to be exempt from tax (allowances) because the income earner is single or married, has children, dependent relatives, life insurance, mortgage or other expenses. The remainder of the income is taxed at so much in the pound, with the last few thousand pounds being taxed at a higher rate than the first few thousand. Both the allowances and tax rate are fixed by the Chancellor of the Exchequer in the Budget.

Most people pay the tax due by Pay As You Earn (PAYE). The income earner fills in a tax form; the Inspector of Taxes then calculates how much tax he should pay in a tax year (6 April to 5 April); the employer deducts the tax, using a tax code given to him, and pays the amount direct to the Inland Revenue.

Income tax, along with taxes on capital (e.g. Capital Transfer Tax on money left after a person dies, and Capital Gains Tax on money made buying and selling shares or property), and taxes on expenditure (VAT), is added to loans to the government and National Insurance contributions. With this money the government is able to pay for roads, law and order, housing, the arts, defence, overseas aid, interest payments on the National Debt, etc.

Questions

1 What can a worker do to be given more pay?   4
2 Apart from money, what other rewards are to be had for work?   2
3 What are the main deductions from gross pay?   3
4 What reasons are there for some workers being paid more than others?   5

Buying and Selling

Money

Money and the Marshalls

Margaret . . . and you see, if we go during the school term time, in May, it's even cheaper . . .

Mum I don't know. It's an awful lot of money Margaret, and there are four of us, and we'd need some spending money as well.

Margaret But, Mum, everyone else is going abroad. Why can't we?

Mum Here's your Dad. Ask him what he thinks.

Dad What's all this, Margaret? We starting up as travel agents?

Margaret Oh, Dad! I just think we should go abroad this summer for a change. Look, here's a cheap hotel and if we go in May it's even cheaper. Think of all the sun and swimming and nightclubs!

Dad Think of all the money, you mean. What do you think, Mum?

Mum Well, it does look nice, and we do have a bit in the bank and if you get your rise . . .

Dad You've started packing already! Let's get some paper and see how much it is all going to cost. Hotel, full board – £145 per person. Half price for children under 13 – that means Jimmy will go for half price, that's always something. So, three times £145 is £435, plus half of £145 is £72.50, so we've a grand total of £507.50 . . . do you think I'm made of money? We can't do it.

Margaret Oh, Dad! Can't we save up? Please.

Mum Yes, Dad, the last time I was abroad was our honeymoon and that wasn't yesterday. Look, you're due a rise, that would help, and I might get a wee job.

Dad All right, all right. My rise will only be £100. Let's see where the rest of this money's coming from, presuming you want to keep paying the rent and electricity, that is.

Mum If we did without chocolate biscuits and coffee and walked instead of taking buses, that might help.

Margaret And I'll do without pocket money, and help Mum bake and cook so we can do with cheaper food. Can we find a cheaper grocer's, Mum?

Mum Maybe, I'll have to think about that. I'll stop smoking though, that'll make a difference. If I put my cigarette money into a jam jar instead of spending it it'll soon mount up.

Dad You'll dip into that quickly enough. Better in the bank or Post Office where you can't lay your hands on it.

Jimmy Can I cash my Premium Bonds to help?

Dad No, better leave them, you might win! But your Savings Bank money might be useful and think of the interest on it.

Mum Let's get it all down on paper. First of all we can work out how much we need to save for the holiday:

Cost of package holiday	£507.50
Spending money	£100.00
Total	£607.50

Now, we need to know how much we have saved up already, counting Dad's rise which we're going to put away.

Bank	£200.00
Post Office	£20.00
Savings Bank	£25.00
Pay rise	£100.00
Total possible savings	£345.00

Jimmy So we're still looking for £262.50. What do we do now?

Dad See how much we spend every month:

Rent	£40
Rates	£20
Electricity	£20
HP	£35
Food	£55
Travel	£24
Pocket money	£20
Clothing	£50
Total	£264

Right, with my monthly income of £270 in my hand, we have £6 left over every month between now and July. It's December now so we might save about £24. That'll not get us far. Now, if we pay the essential bills – rent, rates, HP payments, electricity – could we cut down on the heating a bit? That's about £115 every month we have to pay. Can we try to spend £45 on food, as long as prices don't go up, Mum? We'll all walk and do without pocket money and just £20 for clothes – tights and things like that – that's £84 per month.

Mum We might make Majorca yet! It's only December after all! Maybe we don't need to cut down so much after all.

The Marshalls look as though they are well on their way to Majorca! They were very sensible in looking carefully at their spending and drawing up a budget

Marshall family budget

Where does the money go?

Pie chart labels: Services, Tax Insurance Savings, Alcohol, Tobacco, Furniture and Household Goods, Fuel and Light, Clothing, Transport, Rent and Rates, Food

of all they spent and their total income, then trying to see what savings they could make. They discovered two ways of saving – one was to put whatever money they had left at the end of the month into the bank – that's where the £200 came from; the other is to spend less, by careful shopping, taking advantage of special offers, sales, buying supermarket 'own brands', cutting down on luxuries. They were also very wise in selecting what they could not save money on – they must pay the rent and rates; they must pay electricity bills, though as Mr Marshall began to realise, they might cut down the bill a bit by cutting down on heating.

SAVINGS

Mrs Marshall was not very wise storing her money in a jam jar – not only is it likely to be stolen, but after a year, if she saved £100 she would still have just her £100 – that is if she had not been tempted to spend it! If she had invested it her savings would have earned interest, e.g. if the interest rate was five per cent her £100 would have become £105 by the end of the year. There are many ways she could have invested the money:

In a bank such as the Bank of Scotland, Clydesdale Bank, Trustee Savings Bank, National Savings Bank. They offer a variety of different types of account of which the most common are:
a) a current account, which does not earn interest

(National Giro operates like this) but enables you to pay bills with a cheque or by standing order (the bank sees to regular payments like mortgage and TV rental for you);
b) a deposit account, which earns interest. Some banks have other services – cheque cards, credit cards, cash cards, loans. Some have special rules for withdrawals, e.g. a month's notice.

Save As You Earn is a way of saving a fixed amount each month through the Department for National Savings. At the end of five years' saving you receive a tax-free bonus of a year's savings; if you leave the money untouched for another two years, the bonus is doubled.

Stocks and shares can be bought through a broker on the Stock Exchange. This is a way of lending a company money in return for a dividend (like interest).

Unit Trusts are run by people who invest investor's money in the shares of many different companies. This means the risk involved in buying a company's shares is spread over many companies. Usually the value of unit trusts goes up when the companies are prospering, but if there is a general slump, unit trusts suffer.

Life Insurance involves paying a premium each month and in return the insured or his or her dependants, at an agreed age will receive a fixed sum. There is income tax relief on premiums.

Building Societies lend money on mortgage to people who want to buy a house. They get their money from people who put their money into one of the societies' savings schemes – some are like bank deposit accounts, others involve leaving the money for a number of years. The societies pay interest which is free of income tax.

Advertising

Advertising is the main method by which **consumers** like the Marshalls are persuaded to buy a particular brand of something. It might be a necessity, a luxury, or indeed a type of saving.

The producers want to tell consumers of the existence of their product or to emphasise some new or special quality in their brand of the product. They want to encourage brand loyalty – to make people ask for their brand by name, e.g. 'McPherson's Brown' rather than 'a brown loaf'.

The consumer can compare the range of brands available and pick the most suitable one.

The government makes use of advertisements (£15.5 million a year) and is the third largest advertiser after Unilever and the Imperial Group. The 'Save It' campaign cost £8 million but was estimated to have saved £1500 million worth of energy.

There have been criticisms of advertising on many counts:

the consumer pays for advertising in the end through higher prices;
the consumer can be misled through exaggerated claims or relatively little information;
consumers may be persuaded to buy things they don't really need or want;
our language is spoiled by silly slogans, invented words and changed meanings.

The advertising agencies would reply that:

they give useful information to help consumers choose wisely;
competition between producers and increased sales keep prices down;
adverts brighten up the media and help reduce the cost of the IBA, newspapers and magazines;
advertising is an essential part of a free democratic society.

ADVERTISING METHODS

Where there is no great difference between brands of the same product, the advertising agency must try to come up with a campaign to persuade consumers that their client's brand is better in some way than its rivals. This applies particularly to products such as washing powders, toothpaste and cigarettes, where consumer preference is largely a matter of taste and habit.

Advertisements appear on television and radio, in newspapers, magazines and posters. Apart from free gifts, competitions and special offers, advertisers offer a whole range of less tangible inducements to buy a particular product. They may suggest that if you buy such-and-such a product you will be more popular with the opposite sex or will be seen to be more 'masculine' or 'feminine'; they may use famous people or 'experts' to endorse their product, or produce pseudo-scientific 'evidence' of its merits; they may offer you a whole lifestyle for a few pence, e.g. 'country goodness', 'natural' beauty or old-fashioned cosiness. Or they simply try to associate their brand name with a catchy tune or slogan or image: if you like the advertisement, the chances are you will be well-disposed to the product. It is wise to remember that when you buy something because of an advertisement, you are buying the

advertisement, and to ask yourself if it is really any better than a cheaper version of the same thing. Consumer magazines like *Which?* can help you find out which products are the best value for money.

CONTROL OF ADVERTISING

About £1200 million was spent on advertising of all sorts in 1976. This was almost two per cent of the GNP. There are laws and codes of conduct to regulate advertising and prevent consumers being misled.

Laws such as the Trades Descriptions Act protect the buyer from misleading advertising. Codes such as that of the Advertising Standards Authority (the advertisers themselves) aim to make all adverts 'legal, clean, honest and truthful'. This means that adverts must not break an existing law, offend public decency or morality, or tells lies about their own or rival products.

Television prohibits some types of advertising, e.g. for cigarettes, betting, political or religious groups. Certain techniques are also banned, e.g. subliminal advertising, in which the name of the product is momentarily flashed on the screen and only subconsciously seen by the viewer. Famous personalities are not to be used to advertise products directed at children. Advertising time is limited to seven minutes per hour for television and nine minutes for radio. Adverts have to be obviously separate from the programme and are not allowed at all between certain types of programme, e.g. schools' broadcasts.

Cinema advertising is covered by a broadly similar code but here adverts must be vetted by the British Board of Film Censors and receive similar certificates (U, AA, etc.) as films do.

Posters also have certain standards, but the siting of the billboards themselves is controlled by the local authority planning dept.

Shops

In the past people were self-sufficient – they grew their own food, built their own homes and made their own clothes. During the Industrial Revolution, people became less independent and needed specialists to supply them with what they could not make themselves. Money developed as a useful medium of exchange, instead of barter, and people took the money they earned to shops. In shops they could exchange money for goods produced by other people or firms whom they never saw.

As the system of exchange and industries grew, the numbers and types of shops and other retail outlets grew and changed. The abolition of Resale Price Maintenance brought another change – the opportunity for shopkeepers to charge whatever price they liked for a product instead of having to ask a fixed price, set by the producer.

These different retail outlets, apart from varying in availability, also have advantages and disadvantages depending on the preferences and habits of shoppers.

Type of outlet	Advantage	Disadvantage
Small family business, e.g. Bloggs & Son	Personal service, handy, open all hours	Often expensive, slower service
Volume chain of small businesses, e.g. Spar	Personal service, handy, many own brands, some offers due to bulk buying	Some items may be expensive
Multiple stores, e.g. Saxone	Cheap, high standard, own brands	High Street only, monotonous
Department stores, e.g. Frasers	One-stop (under one roof), luxurious	Often expensive
Self-service supermarkets, e.g. Wm. Low	Self-selection, low prices, loss leaders	Checkout queues, encourage impulse buying, impersonal
Hypermarkets and superstores, e.g. Asda	Self-selection, one-stop, low prices, parking	Remote edge of town site – car needed
Cut-price discount stores, e.g. Horizon	Low prices	Limited range, limited after-sales service
Door-to-door and personal service, e.g. Avon	Convenient, no effort	Pressure from salespeople
Mail order catalogues, e.g. Moores	Convenient, buy at leisure	Impulse buying, cannot see goods

Not all of these outlets are available to everyone and some outlets combine aspects of more than one of the types in the table. Also, different customers will see different advantages or disadvantages. Tastes in shopping may vary, depending on the age, sex, class, character and upbringing of each customer.

Consumer Protection

Since as far back as 1893, the government has tried to protect the consumer against unscrupulous shopkeepers. Today, there is a wide range of legislation giving consumers protection when they buy goods or services. There are also laws to control credit, which make borrowing money for major purchases a less risky business.

Sale of Goods Act (1893) amended by **Supply of Goods (implied terms) Act** (1973), gave the consumer rights in civil law to return goods and get a refund if a) the article was not of a saleable quality, e.g. wouldn't work; b) was not fit for the purpose, e.g. a washing machine that didn't wash clothes; c) did not fit the description, e.g. wrong colour.

Food and Drugs Act (1955 – 1956 in Scotland) concerned food hygiene and the labelling of foods to list the ingredients.

Consumer Protection Act (1961) allows the Secretary of State for Prices and Consumer Protection to make regulations for any type of goods to prevent or reduce risk of death or personal injury, e.g. electrical equipment, toys.

Weights and Measures Act (1963) stated that weight or quantity had to be marked or made known at the time of purchase.

Trade Descriptions Act (1968) made it illegal to describe inaccurately the goods or services offered, e.g. a hotel described as one kilometre from the beach must be that. It also dealt with bogus price reductions.

Unsolicited Goods and Services Act (1971) made it an offence to demand payment for goods not ordered, e.g. sent through post.

Prices Act (1974) allowed the government to subsidise food and regulate the price of food and other household necessities. Shops had to show price ranges and unit prices, e.g. cost per kg.

Consumer Credit Act (1974) controlled the activities of creditors, brokers, owners of hired equipment, debt collectors, etc. Lending organisations had to be licensed by the Director-General of Fair Trading. (A future Consumer Credit Act will force businesses to show the true charge for credit.)

Other bodies have also reached agreements to help the consumer, e.g. under the Fair Trading Act the Director-General of Fair Trading encourages trade associations to draw up codes of practice for member firms. These are purely voluntary and are to improve the traders' standards of service to the customer, e.g. Scottish Motor Trade Association. Newspapers and magazines operate a scheme where a reader will be reimbursed by them if the advertiser (not of a classified ad) goes bankrupt before the customer receives the goods.

Questions

1 In what different ways can the Marshall family save up enough money to go on holiday? 4

2 Which method of saving would you use for each of the following: a) your weekly pay; b) £500 left to you by your aunt; c) £20 a month you manage to save out of your pay; d) money to pay bills; e) money to get married; f) money for retirement? 3

3 What are the main reasons for advertising? 2

4 What are the main criticisms of advertising? 2

5 What methods are used in advertising to persuade you to buy? 4

6 What kind of advertisements are not allowed? 3

7 What would be the best type of outlet for each of the following purchases (give a reason for each answer): a) a loaf of bread at 10 p.m.; b) an OAP's weekly groceries; c) the weekly groceries for a large family; d) a new suit for a farmer living in a remote croft; e) a new washing machine? 5

8 In what ways does the government protect you if: a) a fishmonger's scales are incorrect; b) a toy is dangerous to a young child; c) you receive unordered records through the post; d) a hotel described in the brochure as 'on the beach' is ten minutes' walk from it; e) a pair of shoes fall apart on their first wearing? 5

The Welfare State: Social Wage

Origins and Aims

There used to be a time in Britain when an individual was expected to look after himself, even if a misfortune was not his fault and if others dependent on him suffered as well. For example, a married man with a large family and parents to support, working for a low wage, could have the same income as a single man with no dependents.

There were some voluntary organisations and charities, and some government measures to help him, but it was felt that this was not enough and that the government, or State, ought to do more. Remembering the depression of the 1920s and 1930s, and looking forward to a better society when the war was over, the wartime coalition government set up the Beveridge Committee in 1941. This Committee worked out a plan which first of all identified five main areas of need which ought to be remedied:

Poverty Many people did not have enough money to buy the main necessities of life such as food, clothing and shelter.

Disease Medicine was advancing rapidly, but many people could not prevent themselves becoming ill or disabled, nor could they be cured because treatment was costly.

Ignorance Many children grew up without a proper education because their parents could not afford to send them to, or keep them at, school.

Squalor The living conditions, especially the houses, in which many people lived, were cramped, dirty and lacking in basic amenities.

Idleness A lack of suitable jobs meant that many people were unemployed, and they and their dependents did not have a decent income.

Beveridge said that if all British citizens were to be secure from such suffering, the State would have to look after their welfare, and so he recommended the setting up of a Welfare State which should be:

a) **Universal** – all should be eligible for the benefits provided, regardless of income or other conditions.
b) **Comprehensive** – all likely areas of need should be catered for.
c) **Adequate** – the benefits and services should be enough to provide a minimum standard of life – a 'safety net'.
d) **Normal** – benefits should be provided equally as of right and not as an act of charity.

By 1948, the post-war Labour government had passed the necessary legislation to set up the Welfare State. Successive governments altered the system to improve the benefits and include other deserving cases as their need has become known. We now have a complex system of benefits, allowances, and services which are often said to cover an individual 'from cradle to grave'.

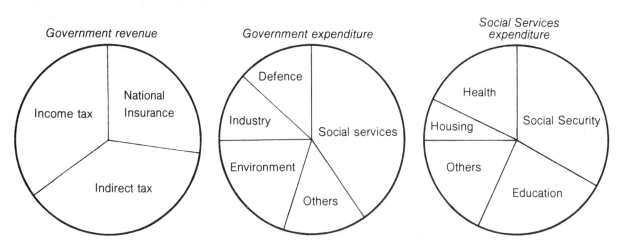

Government revenue

Government expenditure

Social Services expenditure

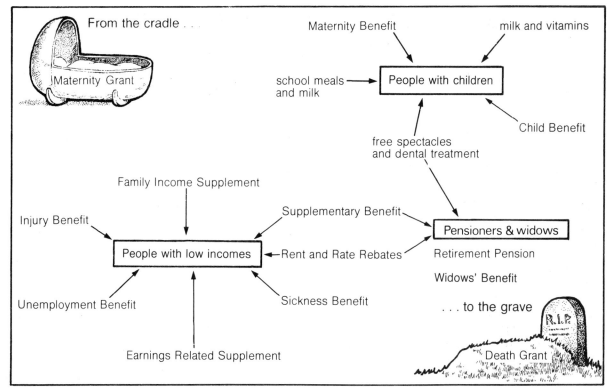

The various benefits available in Britain today

Sources of Money

The money used to pay for the Welfare State comes from two main sources – National Insurance and taxation.

National Insurance contributions are paid partly by the employee, partly by the employer, and partly by the government. There are three main classes of payment:

Class 1 – a worker employed by someone else pays a percentage of his/her wage (say 5¾%) deducted by PAYE and is entitled to all benefits when they apply.

Class 2 – a self-employed worker pays a flat rate (say £2.41 per week) and is entitled to most benefits, though not Unemployment Benefit.

Class 3 – a non-employed person can pay a flat rate (say £2.10 per week) and can claim most benefits though not Unemployment or Sickness Benefit.

Thus some benefits are paid out only to people who have contributed. These include Unemployment, Sickness, Invalidity, Maternity and Widow's Benefits, Retirement Pension and Death Grant. Taxation is required to top up the National Insurance Fund since it is not possible to predict accurately how much money will be required to pay for benefits in the future.

Some other benefits are called non-contributory benefits and are paid to people with special needs regardless of National Insurance payments or earnings. These are paid for out of taxation, and include Child Benefits and War Pensions.

The third type of benefit is called Supplementary Benefit. This also is paid out of taxation. People whose resources are not enough to meet their needs can claim extra money if they can prove that they need it. This is a kind of means test.

Many criticisms can be made of such a complex system. Here are a few:

'The "safety net" is set too low and not enough benefit is given.'

'Some people scrounge when they are not entitled to benefits.'

'The system does not encourage people to find their own solutions.'

'There is too much red tape – too many civil servants, too many and too complicated forms which discourage claimants.'

'Not enough people claim the benefits to which they are entitled.'

'Changes in the system are made too often – either to keep pace with inflation, to correct a flaw in the system, or to fit in with a new government's policies.'

Life on the Dole

Andrew McFadden was made redundant when the local engineering works closed about a year ago. For the first few months he'd been furious. He argued with the staff at the Job Centre and was determined to get a job which he felt his skills as a turner and his long experience deserved. His pride was hurt – he'd done nothing to be put out of work! His family suffered from his bad temper and nothing they could do pleased him.

After six months he'd calmed down a bit. Got used to the routine of 'signing on' and getting 'no thank you' letters from adverts he'd replied to. The woman at the Job Centre was sympathetic, but there weren't any jobs locally. Perhaps if he thought about moving to the east coast, there might just be a chance. But who would move, tear up roots, at fifty, with a family to consider, and an old mother living her years out nearby and dependent on the excellent treatment she got at the local hospital for her heart trouble. There was less money now too. His wife's money from her cleaning job was what kept them above the breadline and bought the kids new shoes. He was for the first time, really grateful that the kids education and schoolbooks were paid for by the State.

He became apathetic after that, felt a failure to himself and his family. He couldn't even get angry and join in the discussion when that young bloke had come to the dole queue with leaflets about a protest march – too much of an effort to go over the same old arguments. He survived on the money he got . . . didn't starve as he would have in the 1930s . . . the government saw to that. Maybe the promised new factories would come . . . he'd just have to wait and see if the jobs came too.

National Health Service

The NHS has become such a large and wide-ranging organisation that expenditure on health in 1976 was £6180 million (compared with £2270 million in 1971 and £388 million in 1949). Eighty per cent of the money to pay for this comes from general taxation and the rest from a proportion of National Insurance contributions and charges for prescriptions, treatment, dentures and spectacles.

The aims of the NHS, as laid out in the NHS Act of 1946 and introduced in 1948, were the provision of a comprehensive health service which would improve physical and mental health and promote the prevention, diagnosis and treatment of illness.

The way in which this was to be achieved was through a whole network of services.

Family doctors (GPs)   There are about 25 000, often working in group practices or health centres, with an average of 2200 patients each. Secretaries can help reduce time spent by the doctor on administration and an appointments system can be organised to save waiting time.

Hospitals   2700 hospitals with nearly half a million beds and over 400 000 nurses, midwifery staff and medical staff.

District nurses, midwives and **health visitors** to attend people needing nursing at home.

Environmental health   Local authorities are responsible for the control of air pollution, inspection of unfit houses, refuse collection, and disposal.

Pharmacies   11 500 retail pharmacies to dispense prescriptions.

Social work   There is liaison between the Social Work Department and the NHS to provide proper care for the handicapped, the elderly, the mentally ill, children and others in need of personal help.

The main problems in the NHS are a result of the shortage of resources due to cut-backs in public expenditure which make it hard to cover the high cost of advanced equipment and medicines. It has also been criticised for the increase in administration and administrative staff compared with medical staff, the regional variations in services available, and the phasing out of existing pay-beds in NHS hospitals.

Questions

1 Give details of the assistance available to Andrew McFadden and his family under the following headings: money; health; education; housing; work.   10
2 Where does the money come from to pay for the Welfare State and what is it spent on?   4
3 What solutions can you offer to the problems of the NHS?   4

Planning for the Community

In a complex society of over fifty-five million people it is inevitable that there will be a need for planning. Its purpose is to provide organisation and order on matters of national and local importance. Planning will normally be the ultimate responsibility of government ministers, local authorities, agencies of government or the nationalised industries. The planners will be concerned with such topics as:

Industry – its location and development.
The economy – governments are concerned with planned policies for economic growth and the solution of economic problems.
Transport – plans for air, road, rail and sea transport are necessary for an efficient allocation of resources and the providing of transport services (perhaps including an integrated network).
Education and Social Services – are planned on a national scale. Matters such as expenditure and the provision of buildings and facilities are planned on a regional or national basis.

The intention of the planner is to examine a subject at the relevant level, consider the needs and demands involved and then offer a long-term development proposal which will meet them. There is, however, the possibility of conflict between the planner and individuals or groups who believe they will be disadvantaged by the long-term development. In the case of local plans, objectors have the right to be heard and a public local inquiry usually gives them the opportunity to present their arguments.

Save Sinclair Street!

James McCourt, 67, has lived in 32 Sinclair Street all his adult life. He has now been told by the local authority that the houses in the street are to be demolished as they are in the path of a link road to the new motorway. This motorway will link two major cities and is necessary for the future economic and industrial development bringing many jobs to the area. Mr McCourt, however, does not want to move and so has refused all the houses he has been offered by the local authority. He has signed a petition calling for a public inquiry and has his speech ready. He only hopes the chairman will be willing to listen though he knows the local authority representative might well tear his arguments to shreds.

Save Loch Doon!

As part of the national development of a nuclear energy programme, scientists wish to begin testing the area of Loch Doon to find out if radioactive waste can be safely buried there. The local authority, on a split vote, have given permission but the local community are totally opposed to any such tests. They are demanding a public inquiry and have staged protest marches, which, because of television coverage, have brought them a lot of publicity and public sympathy.

In such instances the minister responsible has the power to order a public inquiry, but is not bound by the findings. In recent years there have been inquiries on issues such as the building of motorways, and the proposed nuclear developments at Windscale where the planners 'won', and the siting of oil rig construction yards, e.g. at Loch Kishorn instead of nearby Drumbuie where the protesters 'won'.

The following topics – Housing and Environment – are further examples of planning in action. Law and Order is concerned with a more basic form of planning in society.

Housing

In any society, housing is a basic social need and in Britain there are two main types of housing – rented accommodation and privately owned houses.

Rented Accommodation

Tenants rent a house from a local authority or a private landlord or from a specialised agency such as the SSHA (Scottish Special Housing Association). The tenant pays rent to the owner of the house. In the public sector, government, both central and local, has in recent years subsidised these rents, but there has been increasing pressure on them to charge 'economic' rents (i.e. the true cost). In the private sector, the tenant is given protection by law and now has security of tenure, and defence against eviction and harassment. The rent for a furnished or unfurnished private house can now be fixed as a 'fair rent' by

Housing – high-rise flats; old Glasgow tenements; a new housing scheme

independent rent officers (Rent Act 1965 and 1974). Rent tribunals can determine what a reasonable rent should be in properties where the landlord is resident.

Some people argue that councils should be able to sell some or all of their stock of houses to the public. This would reduce the need for a subsidy, would be more efficient, would encourage dwellers to look after the property, and would give more people an opportunity to own their own house. Those against this idea claim that only the best housing would be bought, and that both the quantity and quality of those houses left would decline at a time when waiting lists for such housing are still long.

Private Ownership

More and more people want to buy their own homes. Most newly built homes for sale are bought from private builders, e.g. Wimpey and Barratt. Older properties are usually bought from the owner/occupier, often through an estate agent. Both these types of housing are usually bought by mortgage: Money is borrowed from a building society or local authority for a stated period of time (normally twenty to twenty-five years) at the current rate of interest, and only when the sum borrowed and the interest have been paid back can the owner/occupier be truly said to have bought his own house. Because of interest charges, the total cost over twenty-five years is likely to be at least double the original price. Tax relief can be claimed on the interest paid.

HOUSING PROBLEMS

Within the housing stock in Britain there is considerable variety, including multi-storey flats, tenement flats, four-in-a-block, semi-detached and detached villas, bungalows and cottages. However, in many parts of Scotland there are serious housing problems: Glasgow has more, and on a bigger scale, than almost any city in Europe.

The problem originates in the inner city where much of the housing stock is very old. These houses were not built to the standards and human demands of today. The houses are too small and so there is overcrowding (officially more than one and a half people per room); they lack basic facilities, such as baths, running hot water and internal toilets; they lack planning and amenities, are close to industry and far from open space.

After the Second World War, the planning strategy was to begin a process of demolition. In addition to the problem of cost, this meant that people living in these areas had to be rehoused. To this end, a number of housing schemes were built, often on the outer fringes of the city where land was available. They offered three, four and five apartment houses with modern facilities. Unfortunately, the planners had not foreseen the social problems caused by remoteness and the lack of industry or social facilities. They also had a high percentage of young people with little leisure provision for them, and a general lack of social cohesion. Although there have now been considerable advances these areas are still not popular places to live.

Other housing developments since the war include re-building in older areas where the demolition had taken place (redevelopment) and New Towns — Cumbernauld, East Kilbride, Glenrothes, Irvine and Livingston — run by Development Corporations appointed by the Secretary of State for Scotland. These towns were part of an overall strategy to reconstruct the Scottish economic infrastructure and attract new industries. The population of towns such as Cumbernauld and East Kilbride have a high percentage of former Glaswegians, but in recent years the rapid fall in Glasgow's population has led to a re-examination and there is now an attempt to attract younger people back to the city.

The policy of renovating old housing stock which is still architecturally sound, has become increasingly popular.

Environment

Another topic associated with planning is the social and visual environment. People have become increasingly concerned with conservation, pollution, eyesores and their surroundings in general.

The Social Environment

Any community will need various social and leisure facilities for the various groups and age levels within it. The demands may include a play area, playing fields, a sports centre, cinemas, community centres, theatres, restaurants, and public houses. The provision of such services is intended to allow for leisure and recreation, to offer people meeting places, and to develop social and community identity. This is particularly necessary in areas where people feel isolated from even their neighbours.

Environment and Pollution

Society is increasingly concerned by the evidence of pollution in sea, river and air. In industrial areas, waterways have been polluted by effluent and the atmosphere made dangerous by smoke, fumes and materials such as asbestos. Coastal areas are now threatened by oil from large tankers which collide or break up and leave huge oil slicks, killing birds and fish. Over the years remedies have been sought, such as smokeless zones, laws controlling industrial waste, and the use of materials such as blue asbestos.

"We must refuse your planning application for Rover's kennel; it would detract from the area's pleasant environment."

Air pollution from factory chimneys

The Visual Environment

This is also important. People can be affected for good or bad by what they see around them. This, therefore, raises the need for good architecture and a careful control of all visual aspects of the community. People would rather not see a line of electricity pylons passing through a beauty spot.

The Car Park

The city council have decided that a city centre site which has been cleared will be used to build a multi-storey car park. Those who favour the proposal point out that there is a shortage of parking facilities in the city centre and that an increase in parking meters would further reduce traffic flow. In addition the car park is economically viable and shop owners are sure that their trade will increase. Some councillors, however, are opposed to the proposal on environmental grounds. They argue that cars should be excluded from the city centre wherever possible, since their presence causes noise and air pollution. They also feel that such a prime site could be used to provide a leisure complex. Their final argument is that the design of the proposed car park is unattractive and would not blend with surrounding buildings.

Law and Order

Laws in Britain are made by Parliament. They are called Acts of Parliament and are sometimes added to by local bye-laws, passed by equally democratically elected local authorities. The fact that a law exists does not mean that it will be automatically obeyed by everyone. The law may have to be enforced; suspected lawbreakers captured and their guilt or innocence determined.

The law in Britain is very concerned with the rights of individual people and is prepared to defend both them and their property, within an ordered society. There are times also when society has to be protected from an individual by controls and regulations, such as the Road Traffic Acts.

It is important to note two distinctions:

a) the difference between criminal law and civil law – criminal law punishes people whose behaviour is harmful to the community as a whole; civil law gives individuals rights which they can enforce by suing in the courts.
b) Scotland's legal system is separate and different from the English legal system.

In Britain, as a whole, there is one police officer for every five hundred people. Police work includes the protection of people and property, patrolling and traffic control, crime prevention, criminal investigation, the apprehension of offenders and community liaison. The main departments of the police force are the uniformed department, the Criminal Investigation Department, the traffic department and specialised departments, such as the mounted branch and dog handlers.

In Scotland, the police and other investigative agencies do not determine guilt or innocence – this is the task of the courts. Nor do they decide if a case will be pursued – the evidence is presented to the Procurators Fiscal and they decide whether to go ahead with the case through the courts. It is a basic point of law throughout Britain that any accused is innocent until his guilt is proved beyond reasonable doubt.

When someone has been charged with a crime, the court procedure follows a pre-determined format. The accused will have his case tried in the court relevant to the alleged crime. This is fixed by Act of Parliament and normally depends on the age of the accused (those under sixteen must be referred to a children's panel which is not officially a court of law) or by the seriousness of the alleged crime.

All accused have the right to a defence. If their financial position is below a certain level they are entitled to legal aid, i.e. a defence lawyer whose fee will be paid from the public purse.

In the court all activity must follow the legal and proper procedure. The prosecutor presents his case and witnesses. The defence have the right to question these witnesses. Then the defence have the opportunity to present their case and witnesses who may be cross-examined by the prosecutor. After both sides have summed up, the decision will be made by the magistrate or sheriff. When it is a jury trial, the sheriff or judge will sum up and then await the jury's verdict. (In Scotland the jury has fifteen members, majority verdicts are accepted and they may find the person charged, 'guilty', 'not guilty' or 'not proven'.) Afterwards anyone found guilty may appeal against conviction and/or sentence. Any such appeal will be heard by judges of the Court of Appeal.

The maximum sentence possible for any crime is stated within the relevant Act of Parliament, and the court may not exceed this. Possible sentences include fines, probation, suspended sentences, imprisonment or a period of community service.

Questions

1 What are planners mainly concerned with?   2
2 Write a short speech for James McCourt.   3
3 What attempts could a newly married couple make to get a home of their own?   4
4 What are the arguments for and against the sale of council houses?   3
5 What housing problems has Glasgow faced? What attempts have been made to solve them?   6
6 Describe the different types of housing in Glasgow.   4
7 What are the main kinds of pollutions of the environment?   4
8 What attempts can a planner make to improve the environment?   3
9 Why are there laws in Britain?   4
10 What are the main duties of the police?   4
11 Why do the police arrest but not try; Why does the jury try but not prosecute; why does a judge sentence but not try?   6
12 What parts do the following play in the Scottish legal system: the Procurator Fiscal, a member of a children's panel, witness, police, jury, judge, lawyers, factory inspectors?   8
13 What part is played by Members of Parliament in the legal process in Scotland?   3

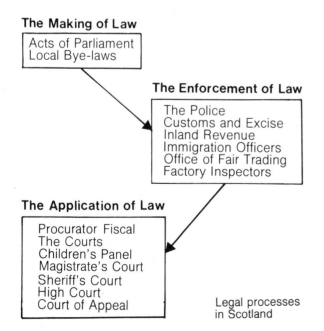

The Making of Law

Acts of Parliament
Local Bye-laws

The Enforcement of Law

The Police
Customs and Excise
Inland Revenue
Immigration Officers
Office of Fair Trading
Factory Inspectors

The Application of Law

Procurator Fiscal
The Courts
Children's Panel
Magistrate's Court
Sheriff's Court
High Court
Court of Appeal

Legal processes in Scotland

Glossary

administration carrying out

authority (local) a group of people with the right or power to control aspects of people's lives

bankrupt unable to pay debts

bureaucracy excessive use of formalities (form-filling) in public business

candidate someone who wants to be chosen for a position or office

collective bargaining negotiations between unions and management about working conditions, wages, etc.

commercial designed to make a profit

community a group of people living in the same area, or the public in general

comprehensive including everyone, e.g. comprehensive school

constitutional related to the laws and principles of government

consumer person who buys and uses goods and services

convention generally accepted way of doing things

debate discussion

declining becoming less strong or profitable

delegate a spokesperson for a group

demand the desire of consumers for goods

deposit sum of money put down as a sign of good faith

devolution the giving of part of Parliament's power to another body (e.g. a Scottish Assembly)

discrimination different treatment of people (usually to their disadvantage)

dispute disagreement

diversification making a variety of products

economic to do with industry and business

economies of scale lowering the cost of items made by increasing the numbers made

election public choice of a person or party by voting

electorate people entitled to vote

environmental to do with the surrounding conditions which affect people's lives

expenditure money spent

facilities specially provided services

grant money given by a government body for a particular purpose

independence having control over own affairs

industrial relations relations between management and workers

industry the making of goods in factories

inflation a fall in the buying power of money (usually seen in rising prices)

infrastructure a system of communications and services which backs up an organisation

insurance money paid against misfortune in the future

integration joining together

interest money paid for the use of money

investment money spent so that more money can be made (e.g. by purchase of a machine)

loan money borrowed to be repaid later

manufacture to make with machines

market a region where there is a demand for goods

media methods of communication

minister a person in charge of a particular department of government

monopoly sole power in dealing with something

multi-national company a huge firm which operates in many countries

multiple deprivation lacking many or all things which contribute to an acceptable standard of life

nationalisation ownership of something by the government on behalf of the people

nationalist one who favours independence for a nation

negotiate to try to settle a dispute

Parliament people who make laws in Britain

political to do with systems of organising

polls the places where people vote

profit money gained from doing business

quorum the smallest number of people necessary for a meeting to proceed

rationalise to organise (an industry) for efficiency and economy

recession a period of reduced activity of trade (e.g. slump)

redevelopment the building of new planned houses, offices, etc. in place of old ones

referendum a vote by all the electorate on a particular question

representative a person acting on behalf of one or more people

resource source of something of value

revenue income of a government

services a useful business or job which does not produce goods

shares equal portions of the capital of a business

social to do with people in groups

standard of living the degree of wealth and comfort which people have in everyday life

subsidised partly paid for by the government

taxation government's method of collecting money from individuals and companies

trade the business of buying and selling goods

vote the expressed choice or decision of people, e.g. at an election